The Life Of Christ

FROM THE GOSPEL OF JOHN

BY FRANK HAMRICK

PositiveAction
BIBLE CURRICULUM

The Life Of Christ

Published 2003

Third printing 2005

Printed in the United States of America

ISBN: 0-9719491-2-3

Adapted by Dennis Peterson
Edited by Ben Wright
Layout and Design by Shannon Brown
Chapter Artwork by Chris Ellison
Photography by Shannon Brown, Frank Hamrick, and Todd Bolen (www.bibleplaces.com)
Charts and Maps by Shannon Brown
City of Jerusalem Illustration by Bill Latta

PositiveAction
BIBLE CURRICULUM

Foreword

Jesus Christ is the unique personality of all time. He has changed the course of history as has no other person or influence. Countless excellent books have been written about the life of Christ, offering huge amounts of information and elaborate essays on chronology and contemporaneous history, customs, and events. Thousands of teachers and preachers have offered innumerable glimpses of the many-faceted life of Jesus of Nazareth.

Yet, sometimes it is still easy to think of Christ as some invisible, impersonal God who is far away somewhere in space. This Bible study on the life of Christ, however, acquaints you with the *visible* and *personal* Jesus, the Christ of God. As you proceed through this study, you will share food with Jesus on the mountainside and laugh with Him at the marriage in Cana of Galilee. As you journey to Jerusalem on the tan grit roads, dust will thicken on your blistered feet and congest your nostrils. Through a dust-choked throat, you will convince Him to rest a little along the way as your muscles wilt from the strain.

You will roam along the coastal area of Galilee, see the soft-colored flowers, and soak up the smell of fresh water from the shimmering sea. And you will rove among the fair maidens, laughing children, and carefree fishermen. You will hear the dogs barking insults at the teasing seagulls. As the azure sky of a sunlit afternoon deepens into the fiery red of evening, you will sleep by His side in a peaceful pasture. You will hear Him rearrange His slumber on the ground at night with a muffled yawn. You will awaken in the middle of the night to the sound of His soft voice speaking to one named Nicodemus.

Then, as you enter the city of Jerusalem with Him, you will see people swarm around and block His way. The sick will throw themselves in His path. They will grasp for His clothing, calling to Him for help: "Jesus! Jesus! Jesus!" Others will hide their faces. You will see His eyes glisten as a smile creases His strong, tanned face.

Finally, your heart will pant and all of your limbs will be seized with shaking and trembling as soldiers come to arrest Jesus and lead Him away as a lamb to the slaughter.

In this study, you will see Jesus as one who lived just as you do today. You will come to Him face to face and heart to heart. You will better know Him personally. This study will cause you to *admire* Him as an individual, to *identify* with Him, and to be *proud* of Him.

The desire of the staff at Positive Action For Christ is that through this study of *The Life of Christ from the Gospel of John* you, the student, will develop a deep *love* for Christ, a sense of His *commission* to you, and a devoted *following* of Him. We pray that your eyes will ever be on that prospect of which He Himself spoke in the very last sentence of John's Gospel: "Till I come."

Features

This student textbook offers several features for your benefit. Preview each of them so that you can take full advantage of them.

Scripture Readings And Recommended Memorization

Each lesson states the exact Scripture passage that you will be studying in that particular lesson. Be sure to read the selected reference(s) carefully and follow it as your teacher presents the lesson. Following this Foreword is a Recommended Scripture Memorization Plan. Follow your teacher's instructions concerning the proper memorization of each verse or passage for each lesson. (Your teacher might ask you to write the text from memory on either your chapter quizzes or unit tests as part of the evaluation process.)

Introductory Readings

Each chapter begins with a brief introductory reading that sets the stage for the material that will be covered in your personal Bible study/lesson research and the teacher's lesson. Read these pages very carefully, paying particular attention to any personal applications that you might be able to make from the material.

Student Work

Each chapter includes a number of questions designed to help you imagine yourself as part of the story of Christ. These questions will help you to put yourself in the place of the disciples, the Pharisees, or the multitudes as you investigate for yourself just who this Jesus is. These exercises may be different from anything you have done before, so don't become discouraged if it is difficult at first. Your teacher will give you more specific instructions and will probably discuss the questions and answers in class. Keep in mind that Scripture does not give us all the answers to all the questions. Some of the other questions will be difficult to answer correctly until after your teacher teaches the lesson. Don't let that bother you, since the purpose of these exercises is not to give you the correct answers right away, but to help you engage your mind to understand what is taking place in the Gospel of John.

Notes From The Teacher's Lesson

Each chapter provides space for you to take notes on the teacher's lesson. Reproduced in your student textbook are duplicates of the overhead transparencies that the teacher will use. As the teacher presents the lesson, fill in the blanks in your textbook, using margins for additional notes.

Assignments And "Fill In The Gap" Sections

Some chapters will include assignments that will require you to study selected Bible references or passages to gather more information on the topic of the lesson. Some chapters will include sections that require you to study some of the other Gospels (Matthew, Mark, and Luke) to gain information about the life of Christ that John's Gospel does not include. Be very careful to complete these sections because this exercise will give you a more complete picture of what Christ did during His earthly ministry and will help you to know Him better.

"Digging Deeper"

At the end of each chapter in the student textbook is a section titled "Digging Deeper." These sections suggest activities for further study that your teacher might ask you to do at his or her discretion. The activities include readings from books, in-depth studies of certain Bible characters or great Christians, creative projects, and other exercises designed to help you take a deeper look at how you can learn more about the topic of each lesson and make practical applications of the major points in the lessons.

Recommended Scripture Memorization Program

Lesson	Scripture reference to be memorized
1	Romans 15:4
2	John 20:31
3	John 1:1–3
4	John 1:10–12
5	John 1:14
6	John 1:27
7	John 1:41
8	John 2:4
9	John 2:19
10	John 3:3, 6, 16–20
11	John 4:13–14
12	John 4:35
13	John 5:8–9
14	John 5:24
15	John 6:5–6
16	John 6:27
17	John 6:35, 37
18	John 7:17
19	John 7:38
20	John 8:12, 32
21	John 9:4
22	John 10:9–10
23	John 10:27–29
24	John 11:25–26
25	John 12:7–8
26	John 12:24–25
27	John 12:46, 48
28	John 13:34–35
29	John 14:1–3
30	John 15:4–5, 7
31	John 17:14–18
32	John 18:36
33	John 19:11
34	John 20:29
35	John 21:22

Contents

Unit 1

Background Information For A Study Of The Life Of Christ In The Gospel Of John

1
An Introduction To The Gospel Of John

All of the other apostles were dead. John was the last of the original Twelve who could give an apostle's eyewitness account of Christ's life on earth. Heresies about Christ were creeping into the church. In light of these facts, John's writings could not only present a true account of what Christ had done, but also combat the false teachings about His life and doctrines.

But John's primary reason for writing his Gospel was different. He stated in John 20:30: "And many other signs truly did Jesus in the presence of His disciples, which are not written in this book…" But his purpose was not to tell *what Christ did*. In fact, John chose to write about only seven of Christ's miracles. Rather, it was to tell *who Christ is*, as is stated in vs. 31: "But these are written, that ye might believe that Jesus is the Christ, the Son of God; and that believing ye might have life through His name."

We are about to embark on a study of one of the most precious, most important, and most powerful books of the Bible. Although the vocabulary and style of writing used by its author are simple, leading some scholars to refer to it as the "simple Gospel," his simple style and elementary vocabulary are a bit deceptive because the Gospel of John is the most profound of the four Gospels. Its message is so theologically deep in some places that Bible scholars have studied it for centuries in attempts to understand fully its meaning and implications, and they still don't know it all.

Various scholars have referred to the Gospel of John as "the heart of Christ." D. A. Hayes called it "the worthy and adequate picture of the life of Jesus among men." A. T. Pierson said, "John leads us past the veil into the Holy of Holies." Jerome said, "John excels in the depths of divine mysteries."

Although the book recounts the events of the ministry of Christ, it also teaches some very profound doctrines that provide the heart of the gospel of salvation. In his Gospel, John states a glorious *principle:* people's souls can be saved by believing in Christ and His atoning work on the Cross. John reveals a glorious *person:* Jesus Christ, the Son of God, God in the flesh. Although this doctrine of the deity of Christ is in the forefront of the book, it does not lose sight of the humanity of Christ. But John's Gospel also shows a glorious *privilege:* one can have eternal life through believing on Jesus Christ.

Other interesting facts concerning the book of John include the following.

- Surprisingly for a book with the deity of Christ as its theme, the name *Jesus* is used more often than the name *Christ.*
- The word *Jew* occurs more than sixty times in John.

- The word *believe* is used more than one hundred times in John, whereas it appears only about forty times in the other three Gospels.

- The word *faith* does not occur even once in John.

- *Eternal life* appears thirty-five times in John but only twelve times in the other Gospels.

The Gospel of John is one of four books in the Bible that depict the life of Christ. Of the four Gospels, John's message is the most profound, its task and purpose the loftiest, and its passages among the most treasured. Before we begin our study of the book of John, however, we must consider some of the background of the book so as to better understand what we do study.

The Date Of Its Writing

The date when the book of John was written has been much disputed. (A sampling of sources indicate the following suggested dates: A.D. 150 "or a little earlier" [Oxford], "late first century" [Thompson], A.D. 90–94 [Jamieson, Fausset, & Brown], about A.D. 90 [Eerdman's Dictionary], and not later than A.D. 85–90 [Unger].) Interestingly, those who think that the book was written sometime well into the second century would eliminate John the Apostle as its author because he would have been long dead! More recent discoveries, however, affirm the date of the Gospel's writing to be during the last quarter of the first century, probably around A.D. 80–90 (see note at right). In fact, the oldest surviving copy of any portion of Scripture is a fragment from John's Gospel.

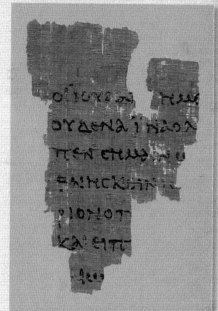

During the 1800s an influential group of liberal theologians in Germany began to question whether the Apostle John actually wrote the Gospel that bears his name. They believed that the book was not written until A.D. 160 or later. In 1934 C. H. Roberts noticed that a small shred of ancient paper in a famous library contained a few verses from John's Gospel. When he studied the style of the Greek writing, he discovered that it matched the style used in Egypt in the first half of the second century (A.D. 100–150). Since John was written from Ephesus, several hundred miles away from Egypt, John's original must have been written some time earlier. This 2.5" by 3.5" fragment, designated "P52," is the oldest surviving manuscript of the New Testament discovered to date, and it provides important evidence that the Gospel of John is an eyewitness account of the life of Jesus Christ.

The Author

 Read John 21:20, 24. According to these verses, who clearly wrote this Gospel? _____

 According to Luke 6:14–16, who were the disciples? _____
_____
_____

(Note that Bartholomew was probably the same person as the man called Nathanael in John 1:45.)

The author of this Gospel was one of those twelve men, but he never used his own name in his Gospel account. We can, however, by process of elimination, determine who the author was *not*.

 Read the following verses and write the names of the disciples who could *not* have written this Gospel:

- John 1:40— _____
- John 1:41— _____
- John 1:43— _____
- John 1:45— _____
- John 6:70–71— _____
- John 11:16— _____
- John 14:22— _____

 Eliminating these men leaves only five possibilities. Who are they? _____
_____

 It must be one of the seven disciples in John 21:2, but of those men, three mentioned by name we have already eliminated. That leaves four, two of whom are identified as the sons of Zebedee. Who are those two men? _____

The other two are simply called "two other of His disciples."

 Read John 21:2–7. Was the disciple whom Jesus loved one of these four? _____

So, this exercise gives us a good idea of who the author of this Gospel was. We conclude that John was the author because he is the most likely possibility among the five remaining disciples. All the historical accounts point to John. The most compelling is that Ignatius knew Polycarp, and Polycarp studied under John. Ignatius wrote that Polycarp said John had written the Gospel.

 Based on your reading of the following verses, record the instances in which the author of this Gospel refers to himself by stating the event, the circumstances, and what he was doing.

- John 1:37–41— _____
_____
_____

(In this passage, the author records the name of only one of the two disciples, the unnamed one being the author himself.)

- John 13:23— _____

    _____

    _____

- John 18:15–16— _____

    _____

    _____

- John 19:16–27— _____

    _____

    _____

- John 20:2–10— _____

    _____

    _____

- John 21:2, 7, 20, 24— _____

    _____

    _____

Predominant Thinking Patterns

To understand the Gospel of John properly, we must understand the thinking patterns of the people to whom it was written.

Gnosticism

Gnosticism (pronounced nos'-ti-sis-im) was a rapidly developing philosophy in John's day. Gnostics believed that God was absolutely good and that matter was absolutely evil. A good God, they taught, could not create evil matter, so there must be other beings descending from God in a chain. These beings were called aeons (pronounced ay'-ons), and each one had a little less deity than the one above it. The last aeon they called Christ.

The Gnostics were divided into two groups, the Docetists and the Cerenthians. The Docetists taught that Christ did not have a flesh-and-blood body; He only *seemed* to have one. The Cerenthians, however, taught that Christ neither was born nor died. They believed that the aeon Christ came upon Jesus at His baptism and left Him at the Cross.

The Mosaic system

The Mosaic system of laws and regulations influenced the thinking of the people of John's day. The Jews followed the Old Testament Law of Moses and rejected the idea that the Messiah would establish salvation for the whole world. Instead, He was to come for only the Jews. This view, of course, explains why the Jewish rulers were so upset at Jesus' teaching that "God so loved the *world* . . . that *whosoever* believeth in Him should not perish but have everlasting life." Such teaching opened the door of salvation to everyone, Gentiles (non-Jews) as well as Jews.

John's attack

In his Gospel, John attacked the popular thinking of the time. In the first eighteen verses of his Gospel, he served notice that both Gnosticism and the reliance upon the Mosaic system for salvation were incompatible with Christian doctrine.

Read John 1:1–3. How did John attack the Gnostic idea of a creator being who was less than God but more than man? _____

_____

How did John answer the Docetic beliefs in John 1:1–14? _____

How did John prove that the Mosaic system was replaced by Christ in John 1:1–18? _____

_____

_____

What did John write about the Jewish belief that Christ was to come for only the Jews? _____

_____

_____

Notes From The Teacher's Lesson

An Introduction To The Gospel Of John

The Place Of John In The New Testament

- One of the four _____
- One of the _____ books of the New Testament
- The_____ book of the New Testament

The Contents Of John

- Different from the _____

- Answers the questions posed by the _____
  - Who is this great King? _____
  - Who is this great Worker? _____
  - Who is this great Man? _____

The Unique Characteristics Of John

- John emphasizes _____ .

- John records only _____ miracles.

- John focuses on Judea rather than on _____ .

- John emphasizes Jesus' own _____ concerning Himself.
  - John is not trying to prove Christ's _____ so much as he is letting Jesus Christ prove his own _____ .

The Application Of The Gospel Of John

- Jesus Christ ought to be more real to each of us, and we should love and admire Him more than ever before.

- Jesus Christ is more than a fact in history. He still lives! He longs for us to know Him, not just to know about Him.

	Matthew	Mark	Luke	John
Portrait of Christ	King	Servant	Man	
Prominent words	Fulfilled	Straightway Immediately	Son of Man	
Written to	Jews	Romans	Greeks	
Emphasis				Deity
Outstanding sections	Sermons	Miracles	Details of Birth and Crucifixion	
Basic characteristics				Spiritual

Digging Deeper

1. Conduct a study of the life of John the Apostle. Specifically, describe his position among the other eleven disciples and his relationship to Christ. Write a brief biography of John. Include in the biography information concerning other books of the New Testament he wrote and the circumstances surrounding them. (You might want to consult such resources as Herbert Lockyer's book *All the Men of the Bible* [Grand Rapids: Zondervan, 1958], pp. 196–197.)

2. Select one major incident in the life and ministry of Christ, then consult a harmony of the Gospels (e.g., Benjamin Davies, ed., *Harmony of the Gospels* [Greenville, S.C.: BJU Press, 1976]), comparing and contrasting the four authors' accounts of that event. Report your findings to the class.

3. Conduct a more detailed study of Gnosticism, describing its major points. Show on a two-column chart how each major teaching of that philosophy is unscriptural. (In the first column, write the belief of the Gnostics; in the second column, write out the verses of Scripture that refute that belief.)

4. Obtain a harmony of the Gospels (such as that suggested in item 2 of this list of activities) for use during our study of John. You will find it helpful in putting together a complete picture of Christ's ministry on earth.

2
The Purpose Of John's Gospel

In this lesson, we probe deeper into the reason why John wrote this Gospel and get an overview of the topics he emphasizes in the book. (You read a little about his reason in the introduction to the preceding lesson.)

The Gospel Of John Proves The Deity Of Christ

Purpose

 John stated his reason for writing the book in John 20:30–31. Why did he record these events? _____

_____

_____

Selective evidence

 John was selective in what he included in his book. According to John 20:30–31 and 21:25, did he record everything that Jesus did? _____

He chose only those signs that magnified adequately the deity of Christ (i.e., the fact that He was God).

 John recorded seven key miracles by Christ. Read the following passages and write down beside the reference the miracle of Christ that John reported.

- John 2:1–11— _____
  _____

- John 4:46–54— _____
  _____

- John 5:1–27— _____
  _____

- John 6:1–14— _____
  _____

- John 6:15–21— _____
  _____

- John 9:1–41— _____
  _____

- John 11:1–57— _____
  _____

Eleven times the Lord used the peculiar phrase *I AM* (the name of Jehovah and a claim to deity). These eleven uses of that phrase or name reveal fourteen different things the Christ claimed to be. Read the following passages and write down what each reveals.

- John 4:25–26—"I AM the _____ ."
- John 6:35—"I AM the _____ ."
- John 8:58—"Before _____ I AM."
- John 9:5—"I AM _____ ."
- John 10:7—"I AM _____ ."
- John 10:11—"I AM _____ ."
- John 11:25—"I AM _____ ."
- John 13:13—"Ye call me _____ ."
- John 14:6—"I AM _____ ."
- John 15:1—"I AM _____ ."
- John 18:5—"I AM He," meaning_____ .

John recorded the testimony of seven people who stated that Jesus was God. Look up each of the following verses. For each verse, name the person who stated Christ's deity and summarize his or her testimony of Christ's deity. (Note: Be sure to distinguish the difference between the person in "a" and the one in "g.")

Reference	Person/witness	Testimony regarding Christ's deity
a. John 1:34		
b. John 1:49		
c. John 6:69		
d. John 10:36		
e. John 11:27		
f. John 20:28		
g. John 20:31		

John Wrote To Cause Men To Believe And Live

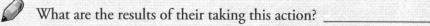 According to John 20:31, what active response must men have to the doctrine of the deity of Jesus? _____

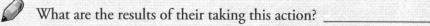 What are the results of their taking this action? _____

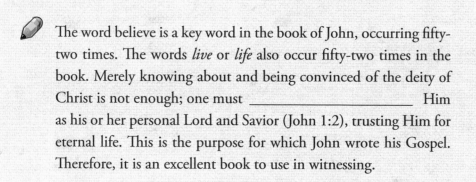 The word believe is a key word in the book of John, occurring fifty-two times. The words *live* or *life* also occur fifty-two times in the book. Merely knowing about and being convinced of the deity of Christ is not enough; one must _____ Him as his or her personal Lord and Savior (John 1:2), trusting Him for eternal life. This is the purpose for which John wrote his Gospel. Therefore, it is an excellent book to use in witnessing.

John Also Wrote To Supplement The Other Three Gospels

The Synoptic Gospels

Matthew, Mark, and Luke are called the "Synoptic Gospels." The word *synoptic* means "to see together." These three books contain much of the same material, even though each book was written for a different purpose.

(Refer to the chart used in Lesson 1 for a comparison/contrast of the various Gospels.) According to *Eerdmans Dictionary of the Bible*, "All three agree extensively in the order of the events they describe" and "in the stories and traditions they share in common." Also, all three of them focus on Christ's Galilean ministry. The book of John, however, supplies information not given in the other three Gospels, thereby complementing, or completing, the biblical picture of Christ.

John was written after the Synoptic Gospels

John was written *after* the Synoptic Gospels. Even where John parallels the Synoptic Gospels, the author includes details not found in the other three Gospels. The majority of John deals with the Judean and Jerusalem ministry of Christ, which is not mentioned in the Synoptic Gospels. (The Synoptic Gospels record only one visit of Jesus to Jerusalem, which is when the Jews crucified Him.) John, however, supplies the missing details, describing four additional visits of Christ to Jerusalem (spring, A.D. 27; spring, A.D. 28; fall, A.D. 29; and winter, A.D. 29) before His final visit there.

John centers on major Jewish feasts

The Gospel of John is built around the major feasts of the Jews. These feasts were the reasons why Christ was in Jerusalem on each of those occasions. These feasts, combined with John's use of the phrase *the next day*, are also good reference points for understanding the order in which the events of the book occurred. John presents the events logically and chronologically and places great emphasis on geographic locations in which the events took place.

John completes the Gospels' scope of Christ's ministry

Taken together, the four Gospels present the entire scope of Christ's earthly ministry in Judea, Jerusalem, and Galilee.

John shows us the time of Christ's ministry

The primary month of Christ's greatest ministry was the period that we call March–April, which the Jews called *Nisan*. Nisan was the first month of the Hebrew calendar (see Neh. 2:1; Esth. 3:7).

The Timeline Of The Book Of John

A timeline and outline of the Gospel of John will help us understand the book. The timeline in the appendix will be helpful as you study through each lesson. Know the eight major divisions of the outline in the chart on the facing page.

The timelines

Found on pages 276–277.

The outline

Topic/event	Scripture passages	Lessons in the textbook
A. Prologue	John 1:1–34	4–6
B. First months of Christ's ministry	John 1:35–2:11	7–8
C. First year of Christ's ministry	John 2:12–4:54	9–12
D. Second year of Christ's ministry	John 5:1–47	13–14
E. Third year of Christ's ministry	John 6:1–10:39	15–23
F. Final three months of Christ's earthly life	John 10:40–11:46	24
G. Last six days of Christ's earthly life	John 11:47–19:42	25–33
H. Resurrection and post-resurrection appearances of Christ	John 20:1–21:25	34–35

Notes From The Teacher's Lesson

The Purpose Of John's Gospel

John's Twofold Purpose

- To cause us to believe that Jesus is the _____ (20:31)

- To show us how to obtain life through His name (20:31)

The Four Passovers

- Passover one—A.D. 27: Jesus is Lord of the temple (John 2:13–14).

- Passover two—A.D. 28: Jesus is Lord of the Sabbath (John 5:1).

- Passover three—A.D. 29: Jesus did not attend (John 6:4).

- Passover four—A.D. 30: Jesus is Lord of life (John 18–19).

The Timeline Of John's Gospel

- The dates of Christ's ministry

  - The first three months (fall of A.D. 26)

  - The first year (beginning with our January, A.D. 27)

  - The second year (A.D. 28)

  - The third year (A.D. 29)

  - The last months (January to March/April, A.D. 30)

- The dates of the events that John records

  - Gaps of time between chapters and verses

  - The bulk of John's Gospel

Lessons For Our Lives

- _____

- _____

- _____

- _____

 Digging Deeper

1. Research and report on the Passover. What did it symbolize? When was it instituted? What did it foreshadow in the ministry of Christ? In what ways is the Passover like the Lord's Supper? (Consult Victor Buksbazen, "Passover and the Lord's Supper," in *The Gospel in the Feasts of Israel* for details on this topic.)

2. Select one of the miracles of Christ for closer study. Describe it and compare/contrast it with other miracles that He performed.

3. Compare and contrast the "I AM's" of Christ.

4. Using the timeline as a basis, prepare a summary of other "secular" events that were occurring throughout the known world at the time of the life of Christ. As part of your summary, explain how the Scriptures (specifically Gal. 4:4) can truthfully say that Christ's first coming to earth was "in the fullness of time." What was going on in the world that made this the ideal time for the appearance of the Messiah?

3

The Geographic And Political Situation At The Time Of Christ's Ministry

Whenever some students see the word *geography*, they cringe, thinking that the subject is boring and impractical. In reality, geography is important for one to understand events of history, especially events in the time of Christ during His earthly ministry. But gaining an understanding of geography can actually be *fun*, too!

Consider, for example, the following interesting facts about one geographic feature of Palestine, the Dead Sea.

- "If a canal were cut to the Mediterranean Sea [from the Dead Sea], the ocean would run in, instead of the Dead Sea running out" (Jesse L. Hurlbut, *A Bible Atlas: A Manual of Biblical Geography and History* [New York: Rand McNally, 1944]).

- It receives more than six million tons of water daily from the Jordan River and other smaller rivers.

- After a very rainy season, it will be fifteen feet deeper and a mile longer than usual.

Size Of Israel

The Dead Sea is one of Israel's most defining physical features. About one-third larger in geographic area than New York City, the Dead Sea is the lowest point on the earth's surface, almost 1,300 feet below sea level. Some factors indicate that the topography around the sea may have changed over the last 2,000 to 4,000 years, and the water level may have been even lower in Abraham's day. It is the saltiest natural body of water on the planet, almost twice as saline as the Great Salt Lake and eight to ten times as saline as the world's oceans.

A rift in the earth's crust makes this region quite unstable. Earthquakes are commonplace. Many Bible scholars believe that God used volcanic activity in this area to judge Sodom and Gomorrha for their wickedness. It is possible that these cities are buried at the bottom of the sea.

The stench of the water is overwhelming due to high concentrations of minerals including magnesium, sulfur, potassium, calcium, and bromide salts that arise from hot springs under the sea. Since the sea has no outlet, the water evaporates, leaving the chemicals behind. Although these minerals have tremendous potential value, it is so expensive to extract them that the resources remain virtually untapped. Drinking the water in any significant quantity can prove fatal, but the taste is so repulsive that the danger is minimal.

- Evaporation is so great that at times it creates dense clouds.

- "The water is nauseous to the taste and oily to the touch, leaving upon the skin, when it dries, a thick crust of salt" (Merrill F. Unger, *Unger's Bible Dictionary* [Chicago: Moody Press, 1967)].

- "It's buoyance is so great that it is difficult to sink the limbs deep enough for swimming" (*ibid.*).

The Gospels are filled with references to other similarly interesting places, all of them connected in some way with the ministry of Christ.

A thorough understanding of the land of Palestine will help one to understand the life and ministry of Christ on earth. Its distinct geographic features and political realities provide the background of His life. Visualizing and tracing His ministry throughout the land enhances our appreciation for what Christ did for us. Refer to each of the maps in the appendix as you progress through this study of the book of John.

Physical Features

The physical characteristics (terrain and bodies of water) of Israel may be divided into five features running eastward from the Mediterranean Sea. List them in the following blanks:

1. _____

2. _____

3. _____

4. _____

5. _____

Jordan River North of Sea of Galilee

What river runs north to south through Israel?_____

What two lakes (called "seas") are found there?_____

Mount Hermon

The Shephelah is the region of gradually rising hills between the coastal region and the Cis-Jordan Hills. Israel has two ranges of hills, the Cis-Jordan Hills and the _____ Hills.

What land region contains most of the cities that Christ visited during His earthly ministry? _____

The highest point in Israel is _____ , which is_____ feet in elevation. Jerusalem is _____ feet above sea level. Just _____ miles from Jerusalem is the lowest point on earth, the Dead Sea, which is _____feet below sea level.

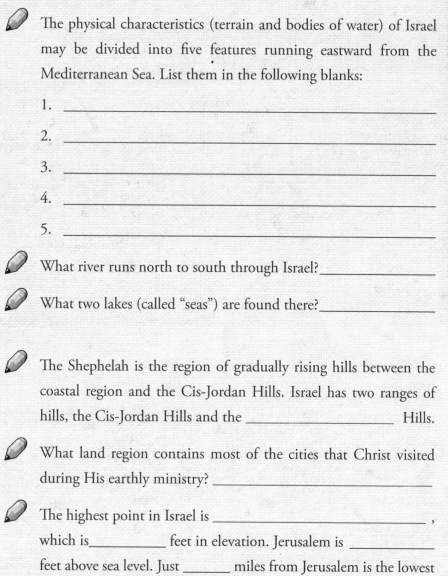

Mediterranean Coastal Plain   Shephelah   Cis–Jordan Hills   Jordan Valley Trans–Jordan Hills

3,000 Feet
Jerusalem 2,680 Feet

S E A   L E V E L

Dead Sea
–1,292 Feet
–2,500 Feet

Scale of Miles

0   10   20   30   40   50   60   70   80   90

Climate

Israel's climate is best described as variable. Extreme differences in altitude in such a small country guarantee widely varying temperatures. When snow is falling in Jerusalem, tourists might be basking under the sun in 90-degree temperatures at the Dead Sea.

Generally speaking, the country has two seasons—warm, dry summers and mild, wet winters. The rainy season lasts from November through March.

The average temperature in Jerusalem ranges from 50 degrees in January to 85 degrees in August. Galilee is pleasant in the summer, whereas the Dead Sea is a scorching 100–110 degrees during that season.

Land Divisions

Palestine comprises three major areas: Judea, Samaria, and Galilee. Other surrounding areas that Jesus visited during his earthly ministry include Perea, Decapolis, and Bashan (see map on page 281).

Widespread ministry

The Gospels mention about twenty-one cities that Christ visited or mentioned by name. Study the map to learn the locations of those cities.

Christ's itinerary

 Following is a list of verses that record parts of Christ's itinerary (schedule of activities). Read each verse and then try to visualize

Christ making the trip by donkey or on foot. Record details about the geography of each place and the mileage involved.

- John 4:1–5— _____

- John 4:43–46— _____

- John 4:54–5:1— _____

- Why did the Bible say that Christ went up to Jerusalem when He actually traveled south? _____

- John 10:40— _____

- John 10:40–11:1–17— _____

- John 11:54— _____
  _____

Political Rulers

During Christ's life on earth, several different Roman rulers governed various political regions of Palestine. The following table lists those rulers, the territories they governed, and the dates of their rule.

Geo-political region	Ruler(s)/dates
Judea and Samaria	Herod the Great (43–4 B.C.) Archelaus (4 B.C.–A.D. 6) **Procurators** Coponius | Pontius Pilate | Ambivius (A.D. 26–36) Rufus | Gratus
Galilee and Perea	Herod Antipas (4 B.C.–A.D. 39) *(Killed John the Baptist)*
Iturea and Trachonitis (northeast of the Sea of Galilee)	Philip (4 B.C.–A.D. 34)

Notes Fom The Teacher's Lesson

The Geographical And Political Situation At The Time Of Christ's Ministry

Location And Size Of Israel

Physical Features

- Climate

- Variety

- Crops

Political Division Of The Land

- Three major areas

- Roman provinces

  - Judea and Samaria

  - Galilee and Perea

  - Iturea and Trachonitis

  - Decapolis

Geographical Divisions

- The Coastal Plain

- The Shephelah

- The Cis-Jordan Hills

- The Jordan Valley

- The Trans-Jordan Hills

Cities

- Christ visited 21 cities.

- Most were located in the Cis-Jordan Hills.

Dead Sea: A Picture Of Many Christians

When fresh water flows in, but nothing flows out . . .

- We lose our joy and enthusiasm.

- We become bitter and harsh.

- We produce no life, and our soul shrivels.

Digging Deeper

1. Report on one of the following geographic features of Israel:
   - Dead Sea
   - Jordan River
   - Sea of Galilee
   - Shephelah

2. Using modeling clay or plaster of Paris, build a scale 3-D model of Israel, showing each of the major geographic features discussed in the lesson.

3. Make a chart comparing and contrasting Israel to *your* state in such information categories as area, population, resources, crops, products, climate, etc.

4. Explain how the geographic and political situations in modern Israel still cause that nation to be the focus of world attention. What is at the heart of the Arab (Palestinian)/Israeli conflict? Using Scripture as your source of information, trace that conflict to its historical roots.

5. Draw a color map of Israel, identifying each of the various political divisions of Palestine during the time of Christ and locating each major city of the time.

Unit 2

Preparations For Christ's Ministry

4

The Preexistence
Of Christ

In the Genesis account of creation (Gen. 1), we read, "And God said, Let *us* make man in *our* image, after *our* likeness . . ." (vs. 2, emphasis added).

Who is the *us* and the *our* in this verse? These plural forms likely refer to the Trinity: the Father, the Son, and the Holy Spirit.

John 1:1–3 states, "In the beginning was the Word, and the Word was with God, and the Word was God. The same was in the beginning with God. All things were made by Him; and without him was not anything made that was made."

The *Word* in this passage unquestionably refers to Jesus Christ, God in the flesh. This passage confirms what the Genesis account says concerning the involvement of the Trinity in creation.

Finally, the apostle Paul wrote of Christ in Colossians 1:16–17, "For by *Him* were *all things* created, that are in heaven, and that are in earth, visible and invisible, whether they be thrones, or dominions, or principalities, or powers: *all things* were created *by Him*, and *for Him*: And He is *before all things*, and by *Him* all things consist" (emphasis added).

Taken together, all of these passages teach two things:

1. All persons of the godhead, including the Son, created all things; and

2. Jesus Christ existed long before His birth in the manger of Bethlehem, even before the creation of all things.

These doctrines are essential to the doctrine of the deity of Christ.

But sinful man does not want to include God in his thoughts, so he invents theories that ignore or try to explain away God's involvement and man's responsibility to Him. Sinful man imagines that all things came into being in a truly mind-boggling and illogical way—by the process of evolution, the idea that all things that are came into being by pure random occurrences over millions (or even billions) of years. It does not matter to sinful man that no scientific, archaeological, or historical evidence exists to support the theory, or that no examples exist of evolution occurring in the present. He ignores the truth so that he can embrace a lie, and then he has the gall to call his theory "science."

Thomas F. Heinz, in his book *The Creation vs. Evolution Handbook*, summarized evolution in this way: "Men have always sought for ways to escape from the knowledge of God, and the thinking man, who does not believe in God as He is, needs some other theory which seems reasonable to him. As long as he can cling to another theory which seems reasonable to him, he feels free to ignore God."

Sadder yet, however, are people who claim to be Christians who are unwilling either to accept God's Word concerning the creation of all things or to reject the lie of evolution. Instead, they try to straddle the fence by attempting to reconcile the two views. In their attempt to seem intellectual and scientific while maintaining the respectability of Christianity, they say that God did create all things, but He used evolution as the tool by which to do it. He created the first life to "set the ball rolling," and then He backed off and let evolution take its course.

The problem with this compromise theory, which is known as *theistic evolution*, is that it is neither supported by the evidence nor acknowledged by either creationists or evolutionists. Creationists reject it because it contradicts the clear Word of God; evolutionists reject it because it includes God, whom they deny.

How much better to take God at His Word. Jesus Christ is God. He existed before all things. He was co-Creator with the Father and the Holy Spirit, and He is the sustainer of all things. In the words of an old hymn, "God said it, I believe it, and that settles it for me."

Student Work

Read John 1:1–13.

✏ What do you think the "beginning" is in verse 1? _____
_____

✏ Jehovah's Witnesses publish a Bible called the New World Translation. It translates John 1:1, "the Word was *a God*" [emphasis added]. This translation violates an absolute law of Greek grammar. How does it affect what people believe about who Jesus is?
_____
_____
_____

✏ John was sent to testify to the light so that all might believe. According to the passage, do all believe? _____ What does this say about the claims of some religious leaders that there are multiple ways to God and that everyone will get to heaven? _____
_____
_____

✏ What are the false ways in verse 13 that people follow hoping to gain salvation? _____
_____

✏ What does it mean in verse 13 that people are born spiritually "of God"? _____
_____

Does this truth say anything about our ability to accomplish salvation for ourselves? _____

Notes From The Teacher's Lesson

The Preexistence Of Christ

The _____ Of Christ's Preexistence

- The doctrine stated by John (1:1)

- The doctrine supported by other Scripture

    - _____
    - _____
    - _____

- The doctrine denied by some

  - An idea in eternity past

  - A man during thirty-three years on earth

  - A memory in the mind of God throughout eternity future

- The importance of Christ's preexistence

The _____ Of Christ's Preexistence

- Distinct from God (1:1)

- Truly God (John 20:28)

- The Creator (1:3)

- Majesty (1:4)

Our _____ In His Preexistence (1:10–12)

- Unknown by some (vs. 10)

- Refused by some (vs. 11)

- Received by some (vs. 12)

Digging Deeper

1. Write a two-page paper explaining why it is important that Christ be both God and man rather than merely God or merely man. Why is this doctrine essential to His deity and His ability to pay the penalty for all our sin?

2. Using a concordance, conduct a study of all of the "I AMs" of Jesus Christ.

3. Read and report on Stanley Rosenthal's book *One God or Three?*

4. Research the theory of theistic evolution. Write a paper comparing and contrasting that theory with the biblical account of creation, and explain your conclusions.

5
The Incarnation
Of Christ

It's the traditional Christmas story.

Little baby Jesus was born in a manger. The angels sang, announcing His birth. The shepherds came and worshipped Him. The star shone brightly over the house in Bethlehem, and the wise men followed it, bringing Him gold, frankincense, and myrrh in worship. Everyone went away rejoicing, but Mary pondered these events quietly in her heart.

We enjoy the story. It gives us a warm, fuzzy feeling inside at the holiday season. We listen to the traditional Christmas carols as we decorate our tree, send out greeting cards, and purchase and wrap gifts for our loved ones.

And then, before we know it, it's all over. Back to the stores go the ill-fitting gifts. Into the trash goes the wrapping paper. Down comes the tree and all of the decorations. Back to the shelves or boxes go the Christmas tapes and CDs. Back to work go parents. Back to school go the kids. Christmas is over for another year, never to be given a second thought—until next year's shopping season begins again, only earlier.

That's how Christmas is for most people, sadly even for many Christians. To them, baby Jesus in a manger *is* Christmas. A baby suddenly appears and causes a brief comforting commotion—and then disappears. And people never give it another thought. The account has no lasting influence on them after December—until the next Christmas season begins.

But is this *really* what Christmas is all about? Or is a more important message in there somewhere?

The story of the birth of Jesus is actually only a small part of the larger story of the life and ministry of Christ. And that relatively brief thirty-three-year life is only a fraction of the larger plan of God for the ages.

The birth of Christ marks what is called the incarnation—God the Son's becoming man so that He could die for the sins of mankind.

Just think about it.

God the Son left the Father and all of the glories of heaven and took on Himself the body of a human with all of its problems and frailties. Or, as Harold L. Willmington put it, "The holy, infinite Creator agreed to wrap flesh and blood around His eternal being, so He might enter this sin-cursed world and eventually die for sinful and finite creatures."

But let's make it personal: He did that for *you* and for *me!*

This lesson is the starting point in fully comprehending the ministry of Christ on earth. We can—and must—study it, but it staggers even the most brilliant Christian minds. Even the apostle Paul found it to be a mind-boggling truth: "Great is the mystery of godliness: God was manifest in the flesh" (1 Tim. 3:16).

It's the true Christmas story that will last believers all year long.

 ## Student Work

Read John 1:14–18.

Verse 14 says that the Word was "full of grace and truth." What events can you think of in the gospels that would show this fullness in Christ? _____

_____

_____

_____

Verse 15 records John's proclamation that Jesus existed before him. What would you have thought about this statement if you heard it and knew John was three months older than Jesus? _____

_____

_____

_____

Verse 16 shows that Christ was not only full of grace and truth Himself, but also shared these gifts with people. How do we receive His grace and truth? _____

_____

_____

Is John implying in verse 17 that grace and truth are *better* than the Law, or just *different*? _____
Why do you think that? _____

_____

_____

Is there anything that Christ was able to accomplish that the Law could not? _____

_____

Bethlehem is located high on a rocky ridge about five miles southwest of Jerusalem. As a small, agrarian community, it is significant in history only because it is the birthplace of David and Jesus. The name Bethlehem means "House of Bread." It is interesting that the Bread of Life was born in the House of Bread.

Notes From The Teacher's Lesson

The Incarnation Of Christ

The _____ Of The Incarnation

- In fleshly form (1:14)

- Not a theophany

- Dwelt among us: comparisons between Christ and the tabernacle

  - Temporary

  - Outwardly _____

  - God's _____ place

  - Where God met man

  - Center of Israel's _____ (Num. 2:17)

The _____ Of The Incarnation (1:14–18)

- To reveal the _____ of God (vs. 18)

- To reveal the _____ of God (vs. 14–17)

- To reveal the _____ of God (vs. 14)

  - The awful consequences of sin

  - God's hatred of sin

  - The consequences that we must pay if we refuse the substitute

Contrary to most modern pictures, the mangers used in Israel at the time of Jesus' birth were most often hewn from solid blocks of limestone. Wood was scarce in first century Palestine, so it was used for more specialized purposes than a feeding trough for livestock. Jerome says that Jesus' manger may also have been formed from mud or clay. Some recent excavations have uncovered inns built near or over caves that were used for housing livestock. This arrangement would have been consistent with the rocky topography of Bethlehem.

Digging Deeper

1. Read Luke 1:26–2:38 and Matthew 2:1–6 (the accounts of Jesus' birth). List the name (or occupation, if the actual name is not given) of the people to whom the birth of Christ was announced. Explain why each received that announcement. Describe the reaction of each to the announcement.

2. Explain in a two-page paper why the virgin birth of Christ is such an important doctrine.

3. Read and report on "When God Becomes Man" in Stanley Rosenthal's book *One God or Three?*

4. Explain ways in which the Christmas story explains and illustrates the doctrine of the Incarnation.

5. What are the consequences of rejecting and/or ignoring Christ?

6. According to the original lyrics of one verse of the hymn "And Can It Be That I Should Gain?", Christ "emptied Himself of all but love." Explain why that statement is unscriptural according to the doctrine of the incarnation.

6

John, The Forerunner Of Christ

Did you ever feel as though you were spinning your wheels, doing a lot but accomplishing nothing? Or do you ever think that you're accomplishing a lot only to find out later that nothing you had done really counted?

Many Christians feel that way about their spiritual lives. They go through the motions of doing what they know they should do but have no sense of satisfaction or accomplishment after everything is said and done.

For example, every believer should read his or her Bible and pray regularly, right? We know that. Doing it is a different story. Even when we get into the habit of doing those things regularly, they sometimes "get old." We get tired of doing them. We continue to do them because "it's the right thing to do," or because we don't want our team in the youth group to lose points, or because we don't want to get into trouble with the youth leader or Bible teacher at school. But we aren't getting anything accomplished spiritually.

This is exactly the feeling about which T. M. Moore was thinking when he wrote, "We've all known them—those seasons when the wind seems to go out of the sails of our spiritual lives. Our time in the Word of God is unexciting and unfruitful. Prayer is a struggle. Worship never quite satisfies. Our devotions are skimpy or even skipped. Our witness is virtually nonexistent. Too many things seem more important than spirituality,

and we would not describe ourselves as 'currently on the cutting edge of Christian growth.'"

Moore calls this predicament "the spiritual doldrums," when "the sails of our spirits go limp while the rest of our life is proceeding full speed ahead." All of this "going through the motions" proves to be what A. W. Tozer called "wasted religious activity." When all is said and done, none of it meets God's requirements because our motives are all wrong.

A similar situation existed in Israel at the time of the ministry of John the Baptist. The Jewish religious leadership was made up of three sects or groups: the Pharisees, the Sadducees, and the Essenes.

The Pharisees were the strictest of the three groups. They formed as a reaction against the religious compromise that was creeping into Jewish society as the influences of Grecian culture took hold under the rule of the Roman Empire. The people were beginning to lose their Jewish distinctiveness, and the Pharisees wanted to bring the nation back to its Jewish roots and fight further decay in society.

To accomplish this, the Pharisees insisted on strict adherence to the Mosaic Law. In fact, they went beyond the Mosaic Law and strongly insisted on strict observance of additional traditions that had been added down through the centuries. They became the religious "nit-pickers" of the day. And because they paid strict attention to the nit-picky rules, they thought themselves spiritually superior to everyone else in society.

Even today in Christianity, some people are not content to emphasize only what God's Word commands. They want to add their own restrictions and then judge people's spirituality more by their adherence to the man-made rules than by obedience to God's Word. This is what one might call modern-day Pharisaism. According to Davis' *Dictionary of the Bible*, "Pharisaism... makes religion consist in conformity to the law, and promises God's grace only to the doers of the law. Religion becomes external." That is, more attention is focused on the outward show of spirituality than on the true inward spirituality.

Tozer believed this attitude of Pharisaism is caused by one of three things:

1. Ignorance of the Scriptures
2. Unbelief
3. Disobedience

Four streams emerge from the melting snows on Mount Hermon and unite to form the Jordan River. The Jordan flows through Lake Huleh and the Sea of Galilee on a route that formed the eastern boundary of biblical Canaan. From Galilee the Jordan empties into a deep rift valley, as illustrated on page 23. This valley drops lower and lower, and the finally Jordan empties into the Dead Sea, 1292 feet below sea level.

The river is typically about 90 to 100 feet wide and from three to ten feet deep. It twists and turns so often below the Sea of Galilee that, although only 70 miles separate the Sea of Galilee and the Dead Sea, this segment of the river itself is some 200 miles long.

One of the topics in this lesson is the way the Jewish religious rulers responded to the ministry of John the Baptist. As you listen to and take notes on the teacher's lesson, examine your own life to see if you have any Pharisaism in you!

And if you want to find out how to get out of those "spiritual doldrums," read T. M. Moore's book *Disciplines of Grace!*

 ## Student Work

Read John 1:15–51. Note the difference between John the Baptist and John the Apostle.

Why did the Jewish leaders send representatives to find out who John the Baptist was? _____

_____

_____

_____

What do you think they wanted his answer to be? _____

_____

_____

_____

_____

Describe in your own words John the Baptist's mission as he states it in verse 23. _____

_____

_____

_____

_____

Why did John the Baptist call Jesus the Lamb? _____

_____

_____

_____

In what way was Jesus like a Lamb? _____

_____

_____

_____

Notes From The Teacher's Lesson

John, The Forerunner Of Christ

John The Baptist In The Spotlight (1:19–23)

- The five questions of the Jewish leaders

- The spiritual condition of the Jewish leaders

    - Spiritual _____

    - Spiritual _____

    - Spiritual _____

- The humility of John

Christ In The Spotlight (1:23–27)

- John _____ himself.

- John _____ Christ.

The Lamb of God in the Spotlight (1:29–34)

- Baptism of the Lamb of God

- Behold the Lamb of God

Digging Deeper

1. Read *Disciplines of Grace* (especially pp. 9–11 and 87–99), and list the solutions that T. M. Moore gives for overcoming "spiritual doldrums" and avoiding becoming like the Pharisees with regard to spiritual responsibilities.

2. Read "The Tragedy of Wasted Religious Activity" by A. W. Tozer (in *A Treasury of A. W. Tozer*), and compare the wasted religious activity that he describes with the Jewish leaders' emphases in Jesus' day.

3. Using a concordance, find and list verses that deal with the need for humility and letting others praise us rather than patting ourselves on the back. Why is this attitude essential to effective Christian service?

4. Conduct a study of feet in the Bible. As part of your report on this topic, explain the principle behind the foot-washing example that Jesus provided for His disciples at the Last Supper in the upper room.

7
The Selection Of Christ's Disciples

Richard was a model railroad enthusiast. In his basement he built a large HO-scale layout modeling the Southern and L&N railroads of the late 1950s and early 1960s. His tiny model world was complete with buildings, industries, people, vehicles, and various types of terrain.

He always kept a sharp eye open for good engines and rolling stock, the various types of freight cars that trains typically pull. He enjoyed watching his model trains glide over the rails around curves, over hills, and through tunnels on the meandering track. His was a *working* layout. He was no mere collector; he wanted to see his trains in operation!

While on an out-of-state trip, Richard visited a hobby shop and found a beautiful black Southern diesel locomotive with gold and aluminum-silver trim. "It will fit perfectly with my layout," he thought as he paid for it.

When Richard got home from his trip, he excitedly ran to his layout room, unpacked his new locomotive, set it carefully on the tracks, and turned on the power pack.

Nothing happened.

He nudged the throttle a little more, sending more electricity through the brass tracks.

Still the engine sat motionless.

Richard gradually nudged the throttle higher and higher. Finally, the head lamp of the engine began to glow. By sliding the throttle a few notches higher, Richard managed to coax the stubborn engine to move, but it did so only in fitful jerks. Only when he moved the throttle to near-maximum power could he get his new engine to move steadily along the tracks.

After tampering with the engine for several hours, Richard concluded that it was hopeless; he could not get the locomotive to perform as he wanted. Sorely disappointed that he would be unable to run the beautiful engine on his layout, he placed it on a piece of track on a shelf in his office. Rather than servicing the imaginary industries in the world of Richard's layout, the engine was relegated to being a mere static display on a shelf.

Similarly, God calls people to serve Him. He purchased them with the blood of His Son on the Cross. He called them to salvation. But then, just as Richard placed his newly purchased engine on the layout and expected it to run, God calls His spiritual children to serve Him.

Although good works or service can save no one, God created us for His service. Ephesians 2:10 says, "For we are his workmanship, created in Christ Jesus unto good works, which God hath before ordained that we should walk in them." God equips His children with the gifts necessary to do the job He has for them, and He expects to see them do it.

Some Christians are obedient to that call. Unfortunately, many professing Christians are not. Although they have been saved, they are unwilling or shallow in their commitment to God in obedience to His call. They prefer, instead, to go their own way, follow their own agenda, and do their own thing. As a result, they do not experience the full blessings of God. They both miss out themselves and also prevent others from benefiting from the blessings that their service could bring.

If you have been called to salvation, God also has another call for you—a call to service. There's a job out there with your name on it. Are you willing to follow God's call, discover the job He has for you, and then do it for His glory?

In this lesson, you will study how Christ called five of His disciples to follow Him. He did not call each of them in the same way, but He definitely called them. Later, after they had obeyed His first call, He called them to serve. Because they obeyed this call of service, the gospel spread around the world—and you enjoy the benefit of their service today.

Student Work

Read John 1:35–51.

When Andrew and another disciple followed Jesus, they called him "Rabbi," or "Teacher." What do you think they expected would happen in their time with Jesus? _____

_____

_____

_____

Simon called Jesus "Christ," or "Messiah." What or who did Simon and the Jews think the Messiah was?_____

_____

_____

_____

What do you think Philip meant when he told Nathanael that Jesus was the one about whom Moses and the prophets had written?

_____

_____

_____

Imagine that you were Nathanael. How would you have felt when Jesus told you that He had seen Nathanael under the fig tree?

_____

_____

_____

Many Bible commentators believe Nathanael was meditating on the Old Testament and perhaps even on the Messiah when he was under the fig tree. It seems likely that Jesus saw him not with His eyes, but through His omniscience. How would Christ's omniscience have been less impressive to Nathanael than the heavenly vision described in verse 51? _____

_____

_____

_____

_____

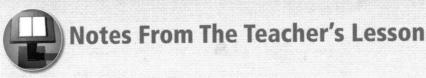

Notes From The Teacher's Lesson

The Selection Of Christ's Disciples

God's Instruments For Witnessing

- _____
- _____
- _____

Lessons For Application

- Different personalities need different approaches.

- Only the Holy Spirit can effectively lead us in witnessing.

"Framing Up" Your Salvation Experience (1:35–39)

Christ's Varying Approach (1:40–51)

- Satisfaction—_____ (vs. 40–41)

- Power to live—_____ (vs. 42)

- Blind obedience— _____ (vs. 43–44)

- Answering objections— _____ (vs. 45–51)

Lessons For Our Lives

- We must approach every believer differently.

- Christ is omniscient and omnipresent.

- He knows our hearts—we can never fool God.

Digging Deeper

1. Read Exodus 12:3–10, 13; Isaiah 53:4–7; 1 Corinthians 5:7; and 1 Peter 1:18–19. Make a chart with three columns labeled "Reference," "Lamb," and "Christ." In the left-hand column list each of the preceding Scripture references. Then, based on these texts, list the characteristics of a lamb in the center column and how each passage compares Christ's life to that of a lamb.

2. Conduct a survey in your church to determine the ways in which various people were saved (e.g., as result of preaching, personal work, circumstances, etc.). Try to discover if there is a pattern between the ways they were saved or the age when they were saved and the types and areas of ministry in your church in which they participate.

3. Refute the "politically correct" idea that "all roads or religions lead to heaven."

4. Conduct a study of Christ's economy of words. What example does that set for the use of our own tongues? List verses that offer advice for how we should use our tongues. How did Calvin Coolidge exemplify this spiritual principle?

5. Based on the definition of *guile* as given in this lesson, what character traits might you expect to find in the life of Nathanael? How does your own life compare with that list of character traits? In which of those traits are you weakest? How can you strengthen those traits in your own life?

6. Read Frances Havergal's book *Kept for the Master's Use*. List and explain the lessons that it contains regarding our call to service.

7. Read chapter 16 of Spurgeon's *Lectures to My Students,* and explain why he believed that it is important to call unbelievers to make a decision about Christ.

Unit 3

Christ's Public Ministry Begins With Individuals

8
Changing The Water To Wine

It's the wedding day! The bride and her mother and friends have planned for weeks—or maybe even months—for this big day. (The groom, as is usually the case, has been relegated to watching all of this planning and decision-making from a safe distance.) Everyone involved in the wedding wants everything to be perfect, to go off "without a hitch." The wedding party has rehearsed everything that is supposed to happen. They've practiced marching in. They've noted exactly where they are to stand. They've memorized their cues. They even know where to stand in the receiving line afterward. Everything is ready for a perfect wedding.

But they didn't count on Murphy's Law: if something *can* go wrong, it *will* go wrong! And despite their best plans and intentions, it does. Any number of things could go wrong, including some of the following possibilities:

- The groom passes out just as the bride reaches the altar on the arm of her father.

- The bride trips over her train as she goes up the steps and falls flat on her face.

- The preacher calls the groom (or the bride) by the wrong name.

- The candelabra falls, setting fire to the carpet.

- The wedding coordinator of the church forgot that a noisy youth activity was scheduled next door to the auditorium at the same time as the wedding.

Cana

JERUSALEM

- The wedding is to be held outdoors, and the weather is rainy, windy, and cold.

- The ringbearer or the flowergirl misbehaves, disrupting the ceremony.

- The best man forgets the wedding band.

- The best man, in transferring the ring from his pocket to the groom's hand, drops it, and it bounces down the air-conditioning vent.

And these are just a few of the innumerable things that could go wrong (and have!) at the wedding. Talk about "life's most embarrassing moment!" At the time such mishaps occur, it's a disaster. Although people in the audience might find these mishaps humorous, other people are embarrassed, perhaps even angered, by them. On this day of all days, everything was supposed to go perfectly, but something went terribly awry.

Jesus also went to a wedding where something went terribly wrong. The Bible doesn't tell us who was getting married, but it says that the wedding party ran out of wine at the wedding feast. That must have been a great social embarrassment to both the families of the newlyweds and the people responsible for providing the party. But Jesus came to the rescue.

In this lesson, you will learn about how Jesus turned this seeming disaster into a spiritual learning opportunity. See how many lessons you can glean from this embarrassing moment.

 ## Student Work

Read John 2:1–11.

What do you think Mary expected to happen when she told Jesus there was no more wine?_____

_____

_____

Why would she have any reason to believe He could or would do anything about it? _____

_____

_____

What do you think Jesus meant by His "hour"? _____

_____

_____

_____

Two types of wine were used in Israel at this time. One type was a strong, highly intoxicating wine. The other type was a weak but sweet drink that was not intended for intoxication but rather to aid in digestion and for refreshment. The fermentation process was used to produce both varieties because it helped eliminate harmful bacteria present in the water. Undoubtedly, it was the second type of wine that was used at this wedding feast, which was served highly diluted. Christ would have had nothing to do with intoxicating beverages because to do so would be a direct contradiction of Proverbs 23:30–32. The phrase mixed wine in this passage refers to the intoxicating variety of wine.

What can we learn from Mary's command to the servants to do whatever Jesus said? _____
_____
_____
_____
_____
_____

The person in charge of the feast said the wine Jesus made was the best of the entire feast. If you were one of the servants, what would you have learned about Jesus by this statement? _____
_____
_____
_____
_____

Verse 11 says this sign manifested Jesus' glory. What do you think His glory is, and how did this miracle show it? _____
_____
_____
_____
_____

What does "His disciples believed" mean? Is this the moment of their salvation, or does it show something else about the growth of faith in the heart of a believer? _____

_____

_____

How would you describe what was going on in their hearts? _____

_____

_____

_____

Notes From The Teacher's Lesson

Changing The Water To Wine

The Time Of The Event (2:1–2)

- Third day—fall of A.D. 26

- Significance of the third day

  - Godhead

  - Resurrection and life

  - Merely a fact

The Ceremony

- The groom comes for the bride.

- They return to his house.

- They celebrate the wedding feast.

The Guest List

The _____ : No Wine (2:3–6)

The _____ (2:7–8)

- Mary's concern: physical and temporal

- Christ's concern: spiritual and eternal

- Christ was the answer.

- The servants' _____
  - Fill the water pots with water.
  - Take the newly created wine to the governor of the feast.
- The Savior's _____

The _____ *(2:9–11)*

- Wine is produced.
- Christ's miracles begin.
- Christ's glory is manifested.

"Christianity does not take the joy out of living. On the contrary, Christianity brings life, and life abundant."—Oliver B. Greene

Digging Deeper

1. Explain and give examples of incidents that prove the truth of Matthew Henry's statement "Man's extremity is God's opportunity."

2. Study carefully John 2:11, which mentions that Christ's glory was manifested by the miracle of changing the water to wine. Record all of the things that you learn about each of the following aspects of the person of Christ in this passage: (a) His power, (b) His relationship with His mother, and (c) how well known He was at that point in His ministry.

3. Note the use of the phrase Mine hour is not yet come (John 2:4). Seven times in the book of John Jesus referred to that "hour." Explain what He meant by that term. Read the following verses (all of which are from John's gospel) and record what was said about "His hour" in each verse: (a) 2:4; 7:30; 8:20; 12:23; 12:27; 16:32; 17:1.

4. Conduct a study of God's timing in various events, both biblical and historical. (A good starting point might be to look up references to "time" or "the fullness of time.") Report your findings to the class.

5. What principles and/or truths about marriage did Christ communicate by His presence at a friend's wedding in Cana?

9
Christ Cleanses The Temple

The temple at Jerusalem was the center of Jewish religious worship. The first such Jewish temple was constructed by Solomon to replace the old tabernacle with a more permanent building. David wanted to construct such a building, but God would not allow him to do so because he had shed too much blood as a warrior (see 1 Chron. 22:8). However, David did collect a lot of the materials necessary for the building and made arrangements to have his son, Solomon, complete it.

Solomon built the temple on the site that David his father had selected—Mount Moriah, east of the city of Zion (today's Jerusalem). To guarantee the necessary space for the temple and its courts, the top of the hill had to be leveled. Construction of the temple began in 956 B.C. and was finished in 949 B.C., so it took about seven and a half years to finish the temple. You can read the details about Solomon's construction and dedication of this great temple in 1 Kings 5:12–6:38; 8:1–66.

Besides Solomon's temple, two other temples have been erected on the same spot. Zerubbabel led the Jews in rebuilding the temple after they came back from captivity (about 520 B.C.). According to the Talmud (Jewish commentaries on the many laws and rules of Judaism), this temple lacked five things that had been in Solomon's temple:

- The ark of the covenant

- The sacred fire

- The Shekinah glory (divine presence) of God

- The Holy Spirit

- The Urim and Thummim (objects belonging to the garment of the high priest by which he learned the will of God in doubtful cases; see Davis' *Dictionary of the Bible*)

The temple of Zerubbabel was plundered and nearly destroyed, but Judas Maccabeus later restored it. Note: Jews today do not consider Zerubbabel's temple to be a second temple, but merely a rebuilding of the first temple.

When Rome conquered Israel, the temple was in grave disrepair. Herod the Great undertook the rebuilding of the temple on a grander scale. The Jews believe Herod's temple was their second temple. Herod's temple took about forty-six years to complete. It was a magnificent edifice and stood until Titus destroyed it in A.D. 70.

Some of the most interesting places in Herod's temple are as follows.

1. Solomon's Porch—the scene of Jesus' famous words, "My sheep hear my voice."

2. The King's Porch (Royal Stoa)—had nearly two hundred marble columns and a high, arching ceiling

3. The "pinnacle of the temple," the southeastern corner of the King's Porch—where the devil took Jesus during His temptation. Doctors of the Law met there to hear and answer questions. It was also where Jesus, as a boy of twelve, talked with the doctors.

4. The Court of the Gentiles—open to all comers, paved with stones of many colors, and where the moneychangers and the cattle dealers desecrated the house of God.

5. The Beautiful Gate—where Peter and John met a beggar and said, "Silver and gold have I none; but such as I have give I thee" (Acts 3:6).

6. The Treasury—where Jesus saw a woman cast in her tiny bit of money two days before His crucifixion.

7. The temple itself—made of white marble; stood many feet above the courts and porches below; gold plates ornamented the front of the temple entrance.

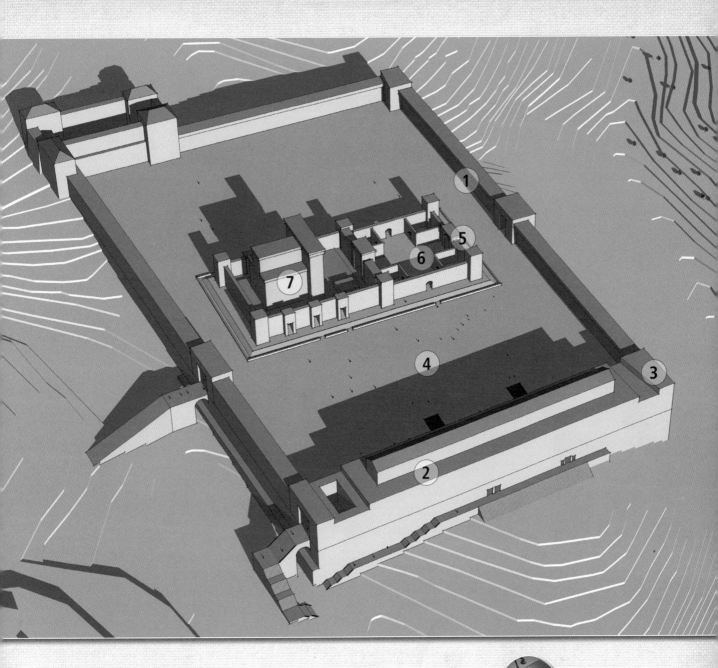

Student Work

 Read John 2:12–25.

 What do you think was Jesus' purpose in going to Jerusalem?

_____

_____

 Did he want to shake up the status quo or merely celebrate the feast? _____

_____

_____

People who sold animals for sacrifice around the Temple provided a valuable service because it was difficult for pilgrims to bring animals with them. Why do you think Jesus got so angry at what was taking place? _____

_____

_____

Verse 22 says that the disciples believed the Scripture after Jesus' resurrection and they remembered what He had said. Does this mean they didn't believe Him before (as in His prophecy in verse 20)?

_____

_____

_____

Is faith in God and His Word a point in time or a progression of growth? Or is it both? _____

_____

_____

Although verse 23 teaches that many believed in His name, verse 24 tells us that Jesus perceived that they were not trustworthy. What do you think Jesus saw in their hearts that caused His skepticism?

_____

_____

_____

What do you think Jesus knew "was in man"? _____

_____

_____

_____

Notes From The Teacher's Lesson

Christ Cleanses The Temple

The _____ ***Of The Event (2:13)***

- The Passover

  - To remind the Israelites of their Egyptian captivity and release (Ex. 12)

  - To be an annual event

- The Jews' Passover

  - Originally "the Lord's Passover" (Ex. 12:11)

  - Degenerated to "the Jews' Passover"

The _____ Of The Event (2:13)

- The _____ and strength of the Lord

- The holiness and _____ of God

- The deity and _____ of Christ

  - Calls the temple "my Father's house" (2:16)

  - Claims He will raise His own body from the dead (2:19–21)

  - Knows all men (2:24–25)

Digging Deeper

1. Study carefully Herod's temple as illustrated in your textbook, then build a 3-D model of it. Apply labels to identify the main areas mentioned in Scripture.

2. Carefully study Herod's temple as illustrated in your textbook. Write a paper as if you were a guide leading a tour group through the temple in A.D. 45. Meet your group in the Royal Stoa (most southern porch of the Temple Mount) and describe what you would tell them as you walk through the porch, cross the court of the Gentiles, pass the barrier, ascend the steps to the Chel, and walk around the Chel to the East Gate leading into the Women's Court. Describe the Women's Court, the Beautiful Gate, the Priests' Court, and the temple itself. As you go through each section, describe what biblical events took place there (if any). For further reference, read _The Temple_, by Alfred Edersheim, Chapter 2.

3. Study carefully the construction and dedication of Solomon's temple (see 1 Kin. 5:12–6:38; 8:1–66). What does Solomon's attention to detail communicate about the quality of the work that was to be done in constructing the temple? What lesson does that have for us concerning the work that we do for the Lord?

4. Read 1 Kings 7:1. What might that verse tell us concerning the direction of Solomon's priorities? What lesson does it teach us concerning our own priorities?

5. Solomon was responsible for the construction of a great deal more than the temple and his own palace. Read 1 Kings 7:2–5, describe what else he built and why. What spiritual effect did this other construction possibly have on him?

6. If Christ visited the "typical" church today, what types of activities or practices might He have to drive out? Why?

7. Today, the body of the believer is the temple of the Holy Spirit. What things might Christ have to drive out of the temple of your body? What practical steps can you take to rid yourself of those problem areas before Christ has to do it for you?

10
Christ Meets With Nicodemus

A shadowy figure moved along the sides of the buildings in the night. The person clearly didn't want to be seen. He moved stealthily between the darkest shadows and ducked through narrow alleyways, avoiding the pedestrians on the main thoroughfares of the city. Whenever he passed someone, he lowered his head and turned his face away from the other person so as not to be recognized. As he walked, he furtively looked for someone, but he didn't want to *seem* to be looking for him.

Finally, the mysterious man saw the object of his search. He waited impatiently until those to whom he had been talking left. Then, when he was sure that no one else was around to see him, he slithered up to the person and addressed him. He might have even motioned for the man to join him in the darker shadows of the night to hide their conversation.

Does this sound like a scene from a spy thriller? Perhaps, but it isn't. It's what it might have been like the night that Nicodemus, one of the leaders of the Jewish religious court known as the Sanhedrin, met with Jesus. But Nicodemus was not like the other Jewish leaders. He had a spiritual hunger and thirst; therefore, he was more attentive to what Jesus said, and—more importantly—he was willing to believe Him.

Why did Nicodemus come to Jesus at night? Some people believe that Nicodemus came to Jesus at night because he was a busy man. His official business as a ruler of the Jews might have kept him so busy that he had no other time to meet other than "after business hours."

JERUSALEM

Other people, however, believe that Nicodemus feared the Jewish leaders so much that he had to meet Jesus secretly. He was certainly risking a lot even to speak to Jesus privately. The Jewish religious rulers hated Jesus and were plotting how they might kill Him, thereby ridding themselves of one who was becoming a thorn in their side. Jesus was widely popular among the common people, He performed miracles, He taught with the force of divine authority—and He threatened their power over the people because He revealed their own hypocrisy. If they had known that Nicodemus was meeting with this vile enemy of the religious hierarchy, they would have turned on him and ruined him professionally and perhaps even physically.

Some Bible scholars believe, as Oliver B. Greene wrote, that "some of the other members of the Sanhedrin were like-minded but lacked the courage to come and talk with Jesus personally. For this reason, Nicodemus became the spokesman for others as well as for himself."

Was Nicodemus a "secret Christian"? If Nicodemus was indeed at this point meeting with Jesus at night because of fear, his fear did not always remain so great. Later, in John 7:50–52, we find him speaking up publicly and officially in defense of Jesus. Granted, his defense wasn't very forceful, but at least he had the courage to speak up, especially considering the fact that it came shortly after someone asked, "Have any of the rulers or of the Pharisees believed on him?" (7:48). His colleagues responded sarcastically, "Are you a Galilean, too?" This was their way of asking, "Do you mean that you've believed on Jesus, too?"

But Nicodemus' courage grew even more over the next year or so. We read in John 19:39–40 that Nicodemus went to the officials to claim the body of Christ following the Crucifixion, prepared it for burial, and put it in the tomb of Joseph of Arimathea. Nicodemus came forth openly and publicly to align himself as a friend of Jesus when all of the disciples had fled for their lives.

If Nicodemus came to Jesus at night in John 3 because of his cowardice, his courage certainly increased over time as he heard Jesus teach, witnessed His many miracles, and saw how He responded to the attacks of the Jewish rulers. His faith grew, and in direct proportion to his faith his courage also grew.

How brave are you when it comes to publicly professing your love for Christ? Are you ashamed to be identified with Him? Do you give in to your fear of others and what they might think of or do to you if they know that you're a Christian, or do you stand boldly for Him? Remember the example of Nicodemus, and grow in your faith and boldness for Christ.

Student Work

Read John 3:1–21.

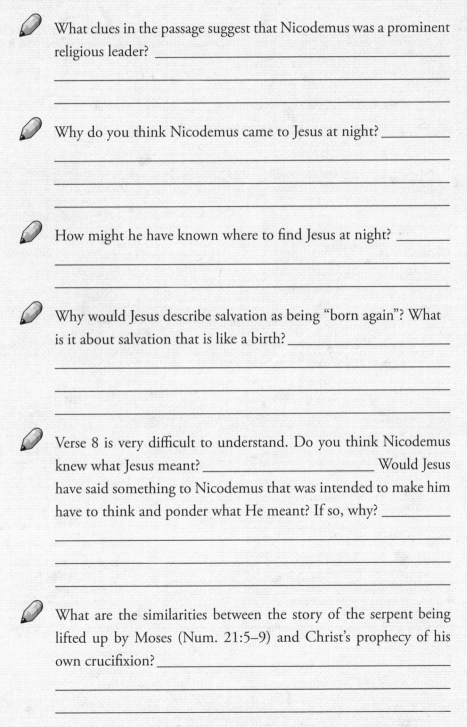

What clues in the passage suggest that Nicodemus was a prominent religious leader? _____
_____
_____

Why do you think Nicodemus came to Jesus at night? _____
_____
_____
_____

How might he have known where to find Jesus at night? _____
_____
_____

Why would Jesus describe salvation as being "born again"? What is it about salvation that is like a birth? _____
_____
_____
_____

Verse 8 is very difficult to understand. Do you think Nicodemus knew what Jesus meant? _____ Would Jesus have said something to Nicodemus that was intended to make him have to think and ponder what He meant? If so, why? _____
_____
_____
_____

What are the similarities between the story of the serpent being lifted up by Moses (Num. 21:5–9) and Christ's prophecy of his own crucifixion? _____
_____
_____
_____

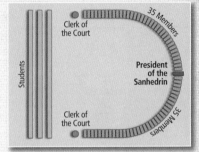

The Sanhedrin was a Jewish ruling body consisting of seventy men presided over by the High Priest. Members included scribes (authorities on the law), elders (prominent laymen), and the highest ranking priests. Their authority included civil administration and law enforcement, but they were also very interested in enforcing Jewish law and traditions. Nicodemus and Joseph of Arimathea were members of the Sanhedrin.

There is some disagreement over the scope and extent of its power at the time of Christ. Some ancient Jewish records indicate that the Sanhedrin was not permitted to pronounce a death sentence, but that only the Roman governor could do so. This record is consistent with John 18:31. Similarly, much has been made of supposed violations of judicial procedures in Jesus' trial before the Sanhedrin.

Some have raised questions about this view because it is not clear whether these regulations were actually enforced during Jesus' lifetime. Stephen's stoning in Acts is a clear case of capital punishment without the involvement of the Roman authorities, but some argue that the Jews may have simply taken the law into their own hands in this case during the absence of a governor. We are left to wonder why the Sanhedrin was concerned about Roman involvement in Jesus' death but not Stephen's.

Regardless of the law, the Sanhedrin's use of false witnesses and Pilate's declaration of Jesus' innocence shows that the rulers in Israel were more concerned about their own power than they were about justice and obedience to God. The Roman crucifixion of Christ was also providentially used by God to involve all mankind--both Jews and Gentiles--in the murder of the Messiah.

✎ Why do you think John focuses on believing in the *name* of the Son of God? _____

_____

_____

✎ What does John say is the key factor in explaining whether people choose darkness or light? What is the motivation for their decision?_____

_____

_____

Notes From The Teacher's Lesson

Christ Meets With Nicodemus

The _____

- A member of the Sanhedrin
- Shows both cowardice and courage
- Educated but spiritually ignorant

The _____

- Miracles as evidence (3:2)
- Miracles and discernment
    - Test of character (2 Cor. 11:13–14; 2 Thess. 2:9; 1 John 4:1)
    - Test of the written Word (Is. 8:20; 2 John 10)

The _____ **: Ye Must Be Born Again**

- _____ of the New Birth
    - First subject Jesus discussed
    - Verbal emphasis (3:3)
    - Only entrance to Heaven
- _____ of the New Birth (3:3–8)
    - Not physical: born "again"
    - Spiritual: "of the Spirit"
- _____ of the new birth
- _____ of the new birth
- _____ of the new birth
- _____ for the new birth (3:15–18)

Digging Deeper

1. Conduct a detailed study of the life of Nicodemus, perhaps beginning your study by reading about him in Lockyer's book *All the Men of the Bible*).

2. Conduct a study of the Sanhedrin. Explain its history, function, famous members, and problems. Report your findings to the class either orally or in a written report.

3. Complete the following chart by reading each of the Scripture passages listed here and writing in the space provided how the physical birth and the spiritual birth correspond. Write the appropriate Scripture reference in the third column beside the respective characteristics. (Scripture references: 2 Cor. 5:17; John 5:24; John 1:13; Luke 15:7; 1 Pet. 2:2; 1 John 4:7; 1 Pet. 1:18–19; 2 Pet. 1:4.)

Physical birth	Spiritual birth	Scripture reference
Produces blood offspring		
Produces offspring who know their parents		
Is forever (once someone's child, always their child)		
Is caused by the parents, not the child		
The child receives the nature of his or her parents		
Produces a baby in need of milk		
Produces a living, growing organism		
Brings joy to the parents		

11

Christ Confronts The Woman At The Well

"He speaks a different language than I do, so I don't like him."

"Her skin color is not the same as mine, so she can't be my friend."

"He talks with a funny accent, so he must be ignorant."

"That nurse is Arab, and Arabs are terrorists, so I don't want *her* treating me!"

"That family's poor; we don't want to welcome them to our church. Why, before long we'd be overrun by a bunch of welfare cases!"

The preceding statements are examples of what is called *prejudice*. *Prejudice* is an opinion or preconceived attitude that is developed and acted upon before one has or understands all of the facts about a person, group, or issue—or sometimes in total *disregard* for the facts. Prejudice leads to hatred toward, intolerance of, and even physical injury to the person or group against which the prejudice is directed.

Remember Jesus' parable about the Good Samaritan? (You might want to read that parable in Luke 10:30–37.) That story illustrates prejudice. A traveler was attacked by thieves and left for dead by the side of the road. First a priest and then a Levite came along and saw the beaten man, but neither of them stopped to help him. Finally, a Samaritan came along. He not only saw the man but also stopped and did everything he could to help him. He provided emergency first aid, we might say, and then he

took him to an inn, where he instructed the innkeeper to provide proper and complete medical care for him. He gave the innkeeper money for that purpose and then said, "If it costs you any more than this, go ahead and do whatever it takes to make him well and then bill me for it."

That Samaritan went out of his way to do so much for the wounded man because he had himself no doubt experienced prejudicial treatment at the hands of others, possibly even priests and Levites. We can assume this because at the time of Christ the Jews despised the Samaritans and treated them prejudicially. In both the parable of the Good Samaritan and the lesson that you are now beginning, however, Jesus taught us that prejudice has no place in the Christian's life. *All* men are sinners in need of God's saving grace, and our responsibility as believers is to share the good news of salvation with *all* men. We are not to hold prejudices that prevent us from sharing the gospel with any group or individual. Once someone accepts Christ, we are to treat him or her as a brother or sister in Christ because there is to be no distinction in the church based on race, ethnicity, national origin, or economic or professional condition.

Does prejudice exist in the church today? Yes. Does that make it right? Definitely not. In this lesson, notice how Christ demonstrated a life without prejudice. How can you follow His example in dealing with your own prejudices? How can you help eliminate the prejudices of others?

 Student Work

Read John 4:1–42.

Why do you think John interjects a comment in verse 9 that the Jews did not associate with the Samaritans? _____

_____

_____

_____

What did Jesus mean by "living water"? What is the difference between the water in the well and this living water? _____

_____

_____

_____

This is an example of a well that would have been used in Christ's day. This well and the watering troughs are located at Tantur.

Why did Jesus tell the woman to go get her husband when He knew she did not currently have a husband? _____
_____
_____
_____

What did Jesus mean when He said that a time was coming when neither a mountain in Samaria nor Jerusalem would be the center of worship? _____
_____
_____
_____

Imagine for a moment that you are the woman. Wouldn't it be embarrassing for you to go into the city to tell the men that Jesus knew everything about you? What would cause you to tell everyone about him so excitedly? _____
_____
_____
_____

Notes From The Teacher's Lesson

Christ Confronts The Woman At The Well

The Occasion: Jesus Departed From Judea (4:1–3)

The Place And People (4:4)

- Between Judea and Galilee
- Populated by a mixed race with a heathen core
- Looked upon with disgust and disdain

The Lord (4:5–42)

- His _____ (vs. 6, 9)
  - Grew weary (vs. 6)
  - Looked like any other Jew (vs. 9)
- His _____ (vs. 14–18, 25–26, 32)
  - Offered eternal life (vs. 14)
  - Omniscient (vs. 16–18)
  - Claimed deity (vs. 25–26)
  - Sustained by spiritual food (vs. 32)
- His _____ and urgency to do God's will (vs. 34–35)
- His _____ for His disciples (vs. 35–38)

Conclusion

- Lessons about evangelism
  - Christ aroused her _____ (vs. 7).
  - Christ made her face her _____ (vs. 13–15).
  - Christ made her see her _____ (vs. 16–18).
- Lessons about salvation (vs. 14)
  - Salvation is a _____ .
  - Salvation brings _____ .
  - Salvation is for whoever will _____ .
  - Salvation is not related to race, wealth, or intellect.

In 1866 a Lieutenant Anderson described the inside of Jacob's Well. He descended through "a narrow opening, just wide enough to allow the body of a man to pass through with arms uplifted, and this narrow neck, which is about 4 ft. long, opens into the well itself, which is cylindrically shaped, and about 7 ft., 6 in. in diameter. The mouth and upper part of the well are built of masonry, and the well appears to have been sunk through a mixture of alluvial soil and limestone fragments, till a compact bed of mountain limestone was reached, having horizontal strata which could be easily worked; and the interior of the well presents the appearance of having been lined throughout with rough masonry."

(The Recovery of Jerusalem. New York: D. Appleton and Co., 1871.)

Digging Deeper

1. Conduct a study of racial prejudice in the modern church. (A good starting point for such a study might be Charles Ware's book *Racial Prejudice and the People of God*. What are the author's main points? Do you agree or disagree with him? Why?)

2. Read and study the lyrics of the song "Fill My Cup, Lord." Where in Scripture did the author of the lyrics get the ideas for this song? What is the central message of the song?

3. Read John 3:22–36; 4:1–42; and Acts 8:5–14 and then answer the following questions.

   - Who preceded Jesus to the villages in Samaria?

   - How did his visit prepare the people for Jesus' visit later?

   - Who followed up Jesus' ministry in Samaria a few years after His visit?

   - How was he received by the people and why?

   - What were the results of his work?

4. Study the evangelistic work of such great men of the Word as George Whitefield and D. L. Moody. What "advance work" was done to prepare the people to receive their message? What steps should churches take in preparation for special meetings? What can individuals do to prepare themselves to receive God's Word during special meetings?

Samaria became the capital of the northern ten tribes of Israel after the nation divided following the death of Solomon. After the Assyrian King Sargon II defeated Israel in 722 B.C., he carried the Jews into captivity and repopulated the land with foreigners. Because these people worshiped the gods of their native countries, God sent lions among them to torment them. Eventually the king sent a priest to teach them how to worship Him, but they merely mixed that worship with their existing rituals.

By the time of Christ, Samaritan worship had been reformed to the point that Samaritans obeyed most of the Pentateuch (Genesis through Deuteronomy), but they maintained their own center of worship on Mt. Gerizim. The Jews hated them because of their mixed racial background and their modifications to the Law of Moses. Many even went out of their way to avoid traveling through that region.

12
Christ Ministers In Samaria And Cana

Tony wasn't the most popular guy or the valedictorian in his high school graduating class. He wasn't a social outcast or a bad student, but neither was he a big man on campus or a member of the honor society. He just sort of plodded along, getting C's and an occasional B. He managed to be accepted into a good Christian college, where he studied accounting and business administration. He sensed a growing desire in his heart to prepare for a ministry in finances with churches, religious organizations, and families who were experiencing financial difficulties.

In college, Tony didn't set any academic records. He struggled academically, but he learned a lot and was doing everything he could to be prepared to serve the Lord when he graduated. During the last few months of his senior year, he interviewed with a Christian financial planning company. Impressed more with his vision and determination to serve the Lord than with his scholastic record, the owner hired Tony to present their services to churches and mission organizations all across the nation.

It took Tony a while to "learn the ropes" of his new employer's programs, but he soon was traveling to churches of all sizes in all regions of the nation, offering assistance in overcoming past and current financial problems, and putting the churches back on the right track so that they could serve the Lord more efficiently with the funds they had. The people to whom he ministered in this way deeply appreciated his expertise, his mild-mannered presentation, and his obvious desire to serve the Lord by helping them. His

company paid him well as a result of his success, and he developed close and lasting friendships with hundreds of people all across the nation.

Then one day his boss told him that he was scheduled to present their program to his home church, which had recently experienced some major financial setbacks when they overextended themselves in a poorly managed building project, and a number of families left the church—taking their money with them. Tony was heartbroken that the church of his youth had gotten itself into such a position, but he was even more determined to help them solve their problem. He visited the church to make his usual presentation, but the pastor was very cool—some people might even say rude—toward him. When he made his presentation, the deacons were clearly reluctant to let him present it to the entire congregation. And when he spoke to the congregation, they rejected his offer of help.

Tony just couldn't understand it. Churches all over the nation had employed his company to help them with similar problems, and each of them had benefited greatly from its services, but his own church coldly refused its help. What had he done wrong?

He reported back to his employer and asked, "Why didn't they let us help them? Didn't I present the message clearly? Didn't I show them the proven results?"

"No, it wasn't any of that, Tony," his boss consoled him. "Do you remember that statement in the Bible about a prophet not being without honor except in his own country?"

"Sure I remember it," Tony replied, "but what does that have to do with this situation? I'm not a prophet!"

"No, but you were returning to your own country, the place where the people remember you only as a zit-faced teenager who barely managed to get through high school. They're too blind to see that God is actually using you to serve Him. They won't let you help them because they don't think that a zit-faced little kid has anything to offer them. They think they know you too well."

Tony thought for a moment about what his employer was saying.

"Jesus Himself faced the same problem," his boss continued. "Jesus worked miracles and led many people to salvation when He preached in Samaria,

but when He went home to Galilee, the people there rejected Him. They couldn't see their Messiah because they were seeing only the son of a lowly craftsman from Nazareth. And that's why your old church didn't accept our offer of help. They couldn't see you as an adult who was trying to minister for their benefit."

Don't be surprised if family, former friends and acquaintances, and other people in your own area reject the message of salvation when you witness. They cannot see you as a messenger of God's Word; they see only what they knew in the past, and for some people that's not a good memory!

So how do you react to such rejection? As Matthew 5:16 commands, "Let your light so shine before men, that they may see your good works, and glorify your Father which is in heaven." Then leave the results with God. If you are faithful in obedience to the Lord, some will accept your message and others will reject it, but you will have a conscience that is clear before the Lord. And remember that Jesus' own people rejected Him, too.

John 4:51 says that the nobleman went "down" from Cana to his home in Capernaum after he spoke to Jesus about his sick son. Cana would have been located behind the individual that took this picture.

The nobleman would have most likely walked across the plateau in the foreground of this picture, then through the pass between the hills. That pass leads into a rift valley that descends several hundred feet below sea level to the plain surrounding the Sea of Galilee. The nobleman would have returned to Capernaum by following the shore of the sea (its left edge in this photo) around to the city on the north side (the top of this photo).

Student Work

Read John 4:31–54.

🖊 What does it mean that a prophet does not have honor in his own country? Can you think of an illustration of this principle that you have seen in your lifetime? _____
_____
_____
_____

🖊 Read the following verses in order, and state what happened just before Jesus left Judea for Galilee and what may have caused Him to leave (Luke 3:19–20; Matt. 4:12; John 4:1–4)._____
_____
_____
_____
_____

🖊 Why do you think Jesus doesn't respond to the ruler's request? _____
_____
_____

🖊 Why does he challenge the man's faith? _____
_____
_____
_____

🖊 When the ruler responds in verse 49, is he ignoring Jesus' challenge, or is he really answering it in a different way? _____
_____

🖊 Why do you think that? _____
_____
_____
_____

🖊 Verse 50 says he believed what Jesus said. Verse 53 says simply that he believed. What's the difference between the two? Is there any difference at all? _____
_____
_____
_____

Isaiah 9:1–2 prophesies of a great light that will shine in Galilee. Now read Matthew 4:12–16. According to Matthew, how was Isaiah's prophecy fulfilled?_____

_____

_____

_____

Notes From The Teacher's Lesson

Christy Ministers In Samaria And Cana

The _____ *(4:31–38)*

- Miss the _____

- Ignorant of spiritual _____ (vs. 32–33)

- Instructed

    - Spiritual vision (vs. 35)

    - Blessings of witnessing (vs. 36–38)

The _____ *(4:39–42)*

- Believe a _____ message (vs. 39)

- Want the Lord to stay with them (vs. 40)

The Miracle (4:43–54)

- The setting

    - Leaving a revival to go to a spiritual _____ (vs. 44–45)

    - Coming again to Cana (vs. 46)

- The nobleman

    - Not exempt from sorrow because of _____
    or _____ (vs. 46–47)

    - Has a _____ of faith in Christ (vs. 47–49)

    - Becomes a believer (vs. 50–53)

- The son: not exempted from _____ by age

Digging Deeper

1. The disciples were learning, growing, and maturing in their time with Christ during the first year of His ministry on earth. List what important lessons they were learning and how.

2. Conduct a study of the educational methods of Jesus Christ. How can a school teacher apply those lessons in the classroom today? How can a youth pastor or Sunday school teacher apply those lessons? How can a pastor apply those lessons?

3. Study 1 John 2:15, then explain the difference between "the world" and "the things of the world."

4. Jesus often went into a "solitary place" to pray. Why was that important? Why is the same thing important for believers today? Do you have a "solitary place" where you can read the Word and pray? If so, describe it.

5. Read "Morning Prayers," chapter three in Matthew Henry's book *Experiencing God's Presence*. List and briefly explain the seven reasons he gives for praying in the morning in a "solitary place."

6. Conduct a study of the man in Mark 2:1–5 who was let down on his bed through the roof. What does that event say about the faith of his friends?

13
Christ Heals At The Pool Of Bethesda

Many people today seem obsessed by an interest in angels. Recently, there has been a widely popular television series called *Touched by an Angel*, numerous Christmas movies portray characters' problems being solved by angels, and both secular and Christian stores feature all sorts of trinkets, jewelry, and other odds and ends that deal with angels. In fact, some people put more emphasis on angels than they do on the Lord Jesus Christ! And not all of these programs or products portray an accurate picture of the role and nature of angels.

For example, in the TV series *Touched by an Angel*, the scripts always have the program end with the angels revealing themselves (and accompanied by a "heavenly backglow") to be angels, whereas in Scripture angels rarely reveal themselves as such. Also, once the angel characters are revealed as such, the characters whom they were supposed to have been sent to help hold them in awe, whereas in Scripture angels never permit themselves to be so adored but rather turn all of the glory and honor to God.

The great emphasis on angels has encouraged some people to treat angel-related objects almost as talismans, or good-luck charms. They seem to believe that if they carry an angel pendant with them or wear a piece of angel jewelry that they will be divinely protected. Such objects become for them like a lucky penny or a rabbit's foot.

John 5 tells of the activity of an angel. The Jews did put a lot of stock in the ministry of angels, and we know that God often used them throughout Scripture. In this particular instance, according to the tradition that had developed, an angel would appear unannounced at odd times and stir up the water in a pool at Bethesda. Whenever that happened, any lame person who managed to get into the water while the waters were being "troubled" would be healed miraculously. We know that this healing was not done in the temple area, which might indicate that it was not officially recognized or sanctioned by the religious leaders. We have no record that they even came to help people get down to the water when the angels troubled it. Did the religious leaders really even care about the lame people who were gathered there in expectation and hope of a miracle?

Notice, however, that when Jesus came to the pool of Bethesda neither did He help the lame man down to the water. Rather, He asked, "Do you *want* to be healed?" The man replied that there was no one to help him get to the water in time. This statement shows the total inability of any man to save another man; salvation must come by God alone.

But Jesus required something of the man in addition to his *desire* to be healed; he had to *obey* Christ's command: "Take up thy bed and walk." The man did not heal himself; Christ healed him. But his obedience brought the blessing whereas Christ provided the power of healing. As Oliver Greene stated, "His obedience *proved* his faith."

How about you? When God commands something of you, how do you respond? Do you react by making excuses, or do you obey in faith? If you expect to receive the blessings of the Lord, you must *exercise your faith by obeying*. Matthew Henry wrote that "those, and those only, can expect to be taught by God, who are willing and ready to do as they are taught."

 ## Student Work

Read John 5:1–18.

Imagine that you are the sick man. What would you be thinking when Jesus asked if you wanted to get well? Would you have expected what was about to happen? Why? _____

_____

_____

_____

The remains of the Pool of Bethesda are visible to-day in the Old City of Jerusalem near the ancient Sheep Market. The pool is about 55 feet long and 12 feet wide, cut from solid rock. A flight of steps wind steeply down to the water. The pool was filled with water that came from a spring nearby. The spring gushed at unpredictable intervals, causing the water to be "disturbed," or to rise and fall. Tradition held that an angel was disturbing the waters, so people thought that those who could get into the water at that moment would be healed. Thus, the Pool of Bethesda became the gathering place for the lame and the blind. The story may reveal the spiritual ignorance of the people in Christ's day.

Over the next several hundred years following Christ's miracle, churches were built over the pool to commemorate the event. As one church was destroyed, another was built to replace it. Tourists today see the remains of a myriad of churches and memorials that mark the spot. The pictures included in this study show what it looks like today.

Verse 13 tells us that the man did not know who had healed him. What do you suppose the man thought had caused him to be healed? _____
_____
_____
_____

Why didn't he ask Jesus who He was? _____
_____
_____

What seems to be the major concern of the Jewish leaders in this passage? _____
_____
_____

Does this surprise you? Why or why not? _____
_____
_____

Some people argue that Jesus never claimed to be God. What evidence do we find in this passage that the Jews believed he was claiming to be God? _____
_____
_____
_____

Notes From The Teacher's Lesson

Christ Heals At The Pool Of Bethesda

The First Year Of Christ's Ministry: A Look Back

- Reviewing what we've studied so far

  - Christ's cleansing of the temple (2:13–25)

  - Christ's meeting with Nicodemus (3:1–36)

  - Christ's meeting with the woman at the well in Samaria (4:1–42)

- Christ's healing of the nobleman's son (4:43–54)
- Filling in the gaps
  - Significance of "after this"
  - Records of Matthew, Mark, and Luke

Christ Reveals His _____ By Healing At A Feast

- The place of the incident
  - Near the _____ gate (5:2)
  - Called _____ (5:2)
- The meaning of the incident (5:2)
- The _____ of the man
  - Impotent (powerless, weak)
  - Blind
  - Halt (crippled, lame)
  - Withered
  - _____
  - Not recognizing _____
  - Needing help
- The _____

Digging Deeper

1. Explain why the Jews worshiped on the Sabbath (Saturday) but Christians worship on the Lord's Day (Sunday). When did the change in the day of worship occur and why?

2. Bible scholars have two differing views concerning the "moving of the water" (vs. 3) by an angel at the pool of Bethesda in John 5:1–4. Some scholars believe that an angel actually did appear at unexpected times and "troubled the water" (vs. 4). Other scholars, however, believe that this was merely a superstition that had developed among the people due to the intermittent gushing of the water from the spring that fed the pool. They believe this superstition illustrated even further the deterioration of Judaism. Research both views and explain which you accept and why.

Unit 4

Christ's Public Ministry
Reveals Who He Is

14

Christ Proves His Deity

The government of Communist China once invited a group of American farmers to tour selected Chinese farms with the expectation that the American farmers could help the Chinese determine what they were doing wrong that prevented their producing bumper crops the way American farmers were doing. They visited the first collective farm on their itinerary and watched as the Chinese farmers tilled their soil in preparation for the planting season. Immediately, the Americans noticed the major reason for the farm's poor production of crops.

"Why, your plows are not set deeply enough," exclaimed one American. He pointed to the tractor as the Chinese driver neared them. "He's just barely scratching the surface. He needs to set that plow deeper."

"How deeply should we set plows?" their Chinese guide asked, his eyes wide with excitement.

"Well, right now that plow's digging only about three inches into the soil," the American farmer replied. "Considering the type of soil you have here…" The America stepped into the shallow furrow made by the plow and sifted the soil through his hands. "…I'd say you should be setting that plow at least a foot deeper. You have to get down beneath the surface and raise up that rich topsoil or your plants won't get all of the nutrients they need. The top few inches of this soil is nutrient poor."

The Americans completed their tour, their Chinese hosts thanked them for their valuable advice, and the two groups parted, the Americans returning to the United States and the Chinese to their collective farms.

A year later, one of the American farmers returned to those same collective farms to evaluate how the Chinese had done in implementing the American advice. He was appalled to learn that rather than experiencing an increase in crops, the Chinese farmers' production had actually declined.

"What in the world happened?" he asked incredulously. "Didn't you follow our advice?"

"Oh, yes!" the commissar of the collective farm said. "We do everything you say. In fact, we do *more* than you say. We decide that if you say set plow one foot deeper and it bring good results, we set plow *twice* that deep and get great results!"

The American farmer groaned and shook his head. "All you did was turn all that rich soil under and bring up worthless subsoil!" he moaned. "You can't expect to raise a bumper crop unless you prepare the soil right!"

When the Jewish rulers contended with Jesus over His claims to deity, He told them, "Search the Scriptures, for in them ye think ye have eternal life: and they are they which testify of me."

The Pharisees, of all people, were definitely Scripture searchers. They dedicated their lives to reading and studying the Scriptures. Yet in all of their study, they were unable to see clearly the truth of what Christ was now telling them: He is God. They thought that through their much study and their meticulous observance of every little rule, regulation, law, and tradition, they would ensure themselves eternal life. But Christ said basically, "You search the Scriptures, thinking that you have eternal life, but you don't really understand what it is you're studying. You're missing the whole point!"

Some Christians succumb to this line of thinking. They believe that as long as they go through the motions of having regular devotions, studying the Bible, and attending Bible conferences that they will be healthy spiritually. But consider carefully what commentator Oliver B. Greene said about such thinking:

"*Scripture* alone cannot make one fit for heaven; *preaching* cannot make one fit for heaven. He who hears the Word *through the preaching* of the Word must allow the Holy Spirit to appropriate the Word and make it part of Him… The Word of God is the life-giving seed, but it must fall on good ground—a willing, open, receptive heart—or it will not bring forth the new birth."

The average professing Christian, however, doesn't even bother to "search the Scriptures." He or she is content to let someone else do that and then give it out in a watered-down, summary format in a Sunday school lesson or Sunday morning sermon. The average Christian is suffering from what one author has called "spiritual anorexia nervosa, a self-induced starvation for the Word of God." Their hearts are not properly prepared to receive the Word, so their lives remain fruitless and barren.

What is the condition of the soil of your heart today? Are you prepared to receive the Word of God as you study it in this lesson? Before you continue with this lesson, why not bow your head and ask God through the Holy Spirit to plow into the soil of your heart and turn up the rich nutrients necessary for the productive reception of His truths?

Student Work

Read John 5:17–47.

 If Jesus' works were simply parallels to what He saw His Father doing, what kinds of works does this passage imply the Father is doing? _____

_____

_____

 Do you think the raising of the dead verse 21 refers to is speaking of physical or spiritual life? _____

 We know that John and the rest of Scripture teach that salvation is by grace through faith. Why does verse 29 connect people's eternal destiny with the kinds of works they do? _____

_____

_____

_____

 There is "another" that bears witness that Jesus' testimony is true. Who might that be? (Keep this verse and question in mind when our study gets into the later chapters of John.) _____

_____

_____

_____

What does this passage teach was the purpose of Jesus' miracles? Was it simply to make sick people healthy?_____

_____

_____

_____

Jesus said that the Scriptures contained testimony about Him. If you were a Jew in this time what would you have thought of when someone mentioned the "Scriptures"?_____

_____

_____

_____

 # Notes From The Teacher's Lesson

Christ Proves His Deity

The Seven Proofs Of Christ's Deity (5:17–29)

- In _____ (vs. 17–18)
- In _____ (vs. 19)
- In _____ (vs. 20)
- In _____ (vs. 21)
- In _____ (vs. 22, 24)
- In power to impart _____ (vs. 24–26)
- In _____ to send men to heaven and to hell (vs. 27–29)

The Four Witnesses Of Christ's Deity (5:32–47)

- John the Baptist (vs. 32–35)
- Christ's own works (vs. 36)
  - His miracles bore witness to His deity
- The Father (vs. 37–38)
  - In the Old Testament Scriptures
  - At Christ's baptism
- The Word of God (vs. 39–47)
  - Testimony to Christ throughout its pages

Digging Deeper

1. Only God has the prerogative to give and take life. Based on this principle, what conclusions can we make concerning the following issues? Does it rule out capital punishment and/or national wars? Why or why not? Be able to support and defend your conclusions with Scripture.

   - Abortion
   - Infanticide
   - Euthanasia
   - Cloning
   - Capital punishment

2. Write a two- to four-page paper explaining why the doctrine of the deity of Christ is foundational to Christianity.

3. Make a chart showing how each of the major false religions and cults of the world deny and oppose the deity of Christ.

4. List the Scripture passages in which John the Baptist testified to the deity of Christ.

15
Christ Performs Two Miracles In Galilee

"Waste not, want not."

"A penny saved is a penny earned."

"Only you can prevent forest fires."

"Make every moment count."

"A stitch in time saves nine."

These statements are examples of proverbs designed to encourage stewardship—the proper use of valuable resources—whether it be time, talents, money, natural resources, or anything else that God has deemed fit to give us according to His grace. They also are good rules for one to follow throughout life—especially for Christians.

Christ taught His disciples an important lesson in stewardship after He miraculously fed five thousand people. He had taken five loaves of bread and two small fishes, blessed them, and had His disciples distribute them to the people. Not only did they have enough food to quiet and satisfy the hunger of every person present but also they had plenty of leftovers. He instructed His disciples to gather the leftovers so that nothing would be wasted. They gathered twelve baskets full of leftovers!

A steward is someone who has been entrusted with something and is expected to take care of it, even improve upon it, until the owner calls for it again. Perhaps a modern-day example will help you understand exactly what a steward is expected to do.

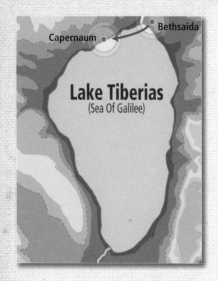

Lake Tiberias
(Sea Of Galilee)

Capernaum
Bethsaida

If your parents have a mutual fund, they are entrusting their money to an investment firm. They expect those financial experts to invest the money in a variety of businesses that will give them a reasonable return on their investment. If the fund manager invests in risky, shady, fly-by-night businesses, your parents could lose all of their money. A good manager, however, will be a good steward of their money, investigating and evaluating each investment opportunity very carefully and buying only into companies with a good reputation and a track record of achievement.

But stewardship begins with the "little" things in life. Jesus said in Luke 16:10, "He that is faithful in that which is least is faithful also in much." People can tell if you are a good steward by such "little" things as how you use your time or spend your money. Someone once said, "Show me a person's checkbook, and I'll tell you what kind of person they are."

Byzantine pilgrims to the Holy Land built a church in the Galilean coastal city of Tabgha. Since they believed the church was located near the site of the feeding of the 5,000, they designed a beautiful tile floor that included a mosaic of two fish and a basket filled with bread. Unfortunately, the location is not near the site described in the Bible, and none of the fish in the Sea of Galilee have two dorsal fins. Ancient Jewish bread was probably not baked with tiny crosses in the center, either.

Do you waste time, life's most precious resource? When you should be studying, are you watching TV or talking on the phone with friends? When you should be in church, are you out enjoying yourself? When you should be reading your Bible, are you doing something else? These seemingly "little" things reveal the degree of your faithfulness in stewardship.

Are you predominantly a spender or a saver/investor? Are you always having to borrow money from others because you've frittered away your own on frivolous things? What do you have to show for the money you spend? Are you spending money for things that will count in the long run? Are you saving money for your college education? Are you investing money in the Lord's work? Are you faithful in giving? Do you give more abundantly as the Lord blesses you financially?

The test of your faithfulness is the degree of your stewardship. Be a faithful steward of *everything* that God has given you—and that's everything! As you study this lesson, note particularly the lesson on stewardship that Christ taught His disciples.

Before we can begin this lesson, however, we must catch up with some things Jesus did that John did not record for us. In His wisdom, however, God inspired the other Gospel writers to record those events for us.

The following table is designed to fill in the historical gap at this point in John's gospel. Read the references in the left column and then complete the table by writing in each of the other two columns where Jesus went and what He did there.

Scripture reference	Where Jesus went	What happened there
Matt. 12:1–8		
Mark 3:1–6		
Mark 3:7–12		
Mark 3:13–19		
Matt. 5–7		
Matt. 8:5–13		
Luke 7:11–17		
Luke 7:36–50		
The following events all occurred on the same day somewhere in Galilee (if mentioned, tell where specifically).		
Mark 3:19–30		
Mark 3:31–35		
Mark 4:1–34		
Mark 4:35–41		

Mark 5:1–20		
Mark 5:21–43		
Matt. 9:27–34		
Mark 6:1–6		
Mark 6:6–29		

As the disciples returned from their tour (see Mark 6:6–29), they reported to Jesus (vs. 30–33). A crowd thronged them so much that they didn't even have time to eat. At this point, John resumed his narrative in John 6.

Student Work

Read John 6:1–21.

What was it about the signs that caused the multitudes to follow Jesus? _____
_____
_____
_____

Were Jesus' reasons for performing miracles the same as the people's reasons for following Him? _____
_____
_____
_____

When Jesus tested Philip, what do you think He was looking for Philip to demonstrate or say? _____
_____
_____

Above is a view of the Sea of Galilee from the Mount of Beatitudes, where the Sermon on the Mount is believed to have been delivered and where the feeding of the 5,000 may have taken place. The view to the left is from the Sea of Galilee looking up towards the Mount.

What would have been the best thing for Philip to say? _____
_____
_____

What did Philip's answer show about how he expected the problem to be solved? _____
_____
_____
_____

When Peter tells Jesus about the boy with a lunch, is he showing faith or discouragement? Explain the reasons for your answer.
_____
_____
_____
_____
_____

What does Jesus' ability to provide food imply about His provision for believers today? _____
_____
_____
_____
_____

Since all the events of the world are moving toward Christ ruling as king of the universe, why did he not let the people crown him king when they wanted to? _____
_____
_____
_____

If you were part of the crowd, what would you have thought when Jesus left? _____
_____
_____

What do you think was Jesus' reason for leaving? _____
_____
_____

Notes From The Teacher's Lesson

Christ Performs Two Miracles In Galilee

The Feeding Of The Five Thousand

- The _____ of the miracle
  - Performed before many people
  - Miracle of creation
  - Picture of Christ
- The _____ of the miracle (6:1–4)
  - During a time of rest
  - Near the time of the Passover

Lessons From Christ's Vacation

- Nothing wrong with Christian workers taking a _____
- Rest from earthly pressure, but be ready to _____ the Lord
- Be _____ to have the vacation end sooner than planned

The Failure Of Philip And Andrew (6:5–9)

- Trials test our _____ .
- Failure is looking at outward _____ rather than God's _____ over circumstances.

The Miracle (6:10–14)

- Reveals Christ's _____
- Requires man's _____
- Shows God's _____
- Reveals Christ's _____
- Shows the _____ that comes from serving
- Reveals Christ's _____

Miracle Of Walking On Water (6:14–21)

- People want to make Him king (vs. 14–15).
- Disciples are in trouble (vs. 16–19).
- The Lord saves the day (vs. 19–21).

Concluding Lesson: Trust In God And Obey His Commands Because He Knows What He Is Doing

Digging Deeper

1. Conduct a study of the questions that Jesus asked of others during His ministry. (For example, in this lesson, we noted that Jesus asked Philip and Andrew a question concerning how they might feed the five thousand people who had been listening to Jesus preach.) Determine and state for each instance (a) of whom Jesus asked the question, (b) His motive for asking the question, (c) why He worded it as He did, (d) the response of the person or group of whom He asked the question, and (e) the result of His questioning.

2. Describe an instance in your life that illustrates the truth of the statement "Every trial that we face is for the same reason. Trials do not come by accident; there are no accidents with God. They are all arranged by the Lord to test our faith." Did you pass the test? What did you learn from the experience?

3. What principles about orderliness can you glean from the account of how Christ fed the five thousand? How can you apply them to your own situation today?

4. One lesson that Christ taught the disciples during His feeding of the five thousand was that of proper stewardship of resources. Explain how He taught that principle, and list practical ways in which you can apply the same principle today.

5. Read and report on the contents of a good book on Christian stewardship of finances (for example, James L. Paris' book *Money Management for Those Who Don't Have Any*). List ways in which you as a student can already put those ideas into practice, thereby becoming a better steward of the money with which the Lord has entrusted you.

6. Read a book on time management. (Examples include such titles as *Managing Your Time* by Engstrom and MacKenzie, *Christian Time Management* by Erickson, *A Workshop on Time Management* by Roecker, and *How to Balance Competing Time Demands* by Sherman and Hendricks.) List ideas that you can apply now that will make you a better steward of your time.

7. Keep a journal of your use of time for one week (or month). Make a chart that breaks each day into fifteen-minute increments. Write down how you spent each of those segments of time during the week (or month). What conclusions can you make from your findings? What changes might you make to improve your stewardship of time?

16
Christ Teaches That He Is The Bread Of Life
(Part 1)

"The weather map shows a very strong cold front heading down from Canada and a warm front streaming up from the Gulf of Mexico," the TV meteorologist declares with a serious look. "Depending on where these two fronts meet, our region could be in for some significant snowfall."

Suddenly, all viewers are alert. Even those who have been trying to do homework with the TV blaring are suddenly all ears.

"Yes, we could very well be in for a heavy snowfall in the viewing area," the forecaster continues. "The National Weather Service has issued a severe winter storm alert for the entire region, and we're calling for snowfall amounts to be in double digits. Stayed tuned for the latest details about this approaching storm at eleven."

You'd better believe that viewers will be glued to their TV sets when the eleven o'clock news comes on. But between the evening news and the eleven o'clock news, they have to do something very important.

In the regions of the United States that have snowstorms, even the hint of such a forecast of snow can create a rush on the supermarkets. People fear being trapped in their houses by a record snowfall without the basic necessities of life. As a result, the stores are jammed with shoppers. Very quickly, the shelves are bare in aisles where bread, milk, and toilet paper are normally plentiful.

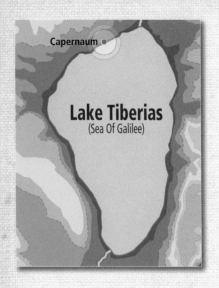

Capernaum

Lake Tiberias
(Sea Of Galilee)

Like water, bread is a staple of life. In fact, the very word *bread* is symbolic of sustenance and subsistence. It is representative of the basic requirement of life.

When Christ taught His disciples to pray, He said that they should pray thus to the Father, "Give us this day our daily bread." By this, He showed that we are dependent upon God for even the bare essentials of life.

In this lesson and the next, we will study Christ's claim that He is the Bread of Life, the essential aspect of a proper spiritual diet. Without Him, our souls are famished, just as our physical bodies are starved unless we have bread to eat. But that spiritual bread is even more important as we face the storms of life and the attacks of Satan.

As we study these two lessons, pay particular attention to Christ's role as the Bread of Life. Note ways in which He meets your most basic needs.

Student Work

Read John 6:22–32.

Since the crowds knew Jesus had not gone into the boat, how do you suppose they thought He got to the other side of the lake?

_____

_____

_____

What other questions might have been going through their minds about Jesus at this time? _____

_____

_____

What does Jesus' answer to them in verse 26 suggest about what He knew was in their hearts? _____

_____

_____

Were the people focusing on the food or the power that produced it? _____

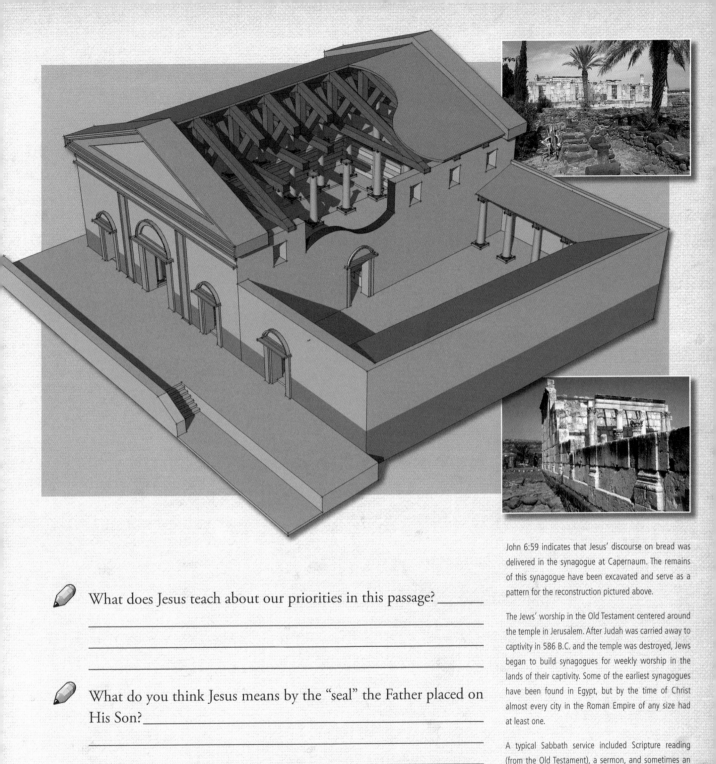

What does Jesus teach about our priorities in this passage? _____
_____
_____
_____

What do you think Jesus means by the "seal" the Father placed on His Son? _____
_____
_____
_____

What does Jesus show the crowds in verses 27–30 about man's inability to please God? _____
_____
_____
_____

John 6:59 indicates that Jesus' discourse on bread was delivered in the synagogue at Capernaum. The remains of this synagogue have been excavated and serve as a pattern for the reconstruction pictured above.

The Jews' worship in the Old Testament centered around the temple in Jerusalem. After Judah was carried away to captivity in 586 B.C. and the temple was destroyed, Jews began to build synagogues for weekly worship in the lands of their captivity. Some of the earliest synagogues have been found in Egypt, but by the time of Christ almost every city in the Roman Empire of any size had at least one.

A typical Sabbath service included Scripture reading (from the Old Testament), a sermon, and sometimes an opportunity for the adult men to ask questions. See Luke 4:16–30 for a description of a Sabbath meeting in which Jesus participated.

What is the only "work" one can do that pleases God? _____
_____
_____
_____
_____

How is the "work" of belief different from the works about which
the people were asking? _____
_____
_____
_____

Is verse 30 a reasonable question? _____

What are the people in the crowd forgetting? _____
_____
_____
_____

Notes From The Teacher's Lesson

Christ Teaches That He Is The Bread Of Life (Part 1)

The Setting (6:22–25)

- The place: the _____ of Capernaum (vs. 59)

- The time: _____ the feeding of the five thousand

The Command (6:26–39)

- His _____ : knows why they
  sought Him (vs. 26)

- His _____: pursue spiritual
  realities, not temporal goals (vs. 27)

- The _____ : Jews believe salvation
  is by works (vs. 28)

- The _____ : only "work" is to
  believe in Christ (vs. 29)

The Unbelief: Looking For A Sign (6:30–32)

Digging Deeper

1. Read John 6:27. Give examples of the "meat which perisheth" that Christian young people are often guilty of pursuing. Which of these things are you tempted to chase? List steps by which you can push these things into the background of your life and put the more important things of the Lord's work first.

2. What are the right reasons for serving the Lord? What steps can you take to ensure that you maintain the right reasons and motives in your life? How can you keep the right priorities in life, ensuring that you put "first things first"?

3. Study other bread- or baking-related comments that Christ made in Scripture. (For example, Christ warned His disciples about "the leaven of the Pharisees.") What did He mean? How do such comments relate directly to your life?

4. One activity in the preceding chapter asked you to study the questions that Christ asked of others. For this chapter, conduct a study of the questions that other people asked of Christ. Determine and state for each instance (a) the specific question asked, (b) who asked Jesus the question, (c) the person's motive for asking the question, (d) Christ's response to the question, (d) the reaction of the person who had asked the question, and (e) the lesson(s) that Christ's answer taught the person.

5. Make a chart showing the major false religions and cults of the world, and list the different works that each requires for salvation. Using Scripture, refute each such false teaching.

6. Explain why man insists on receiving or seeing a "sign" before he will believe. How do visible means of portraying God lead to idolatry? Give examples, both from Scripture and history, of how this has happened. What steps has God often taken to ensure that His people do not fall into the trap of idolizing various objects?

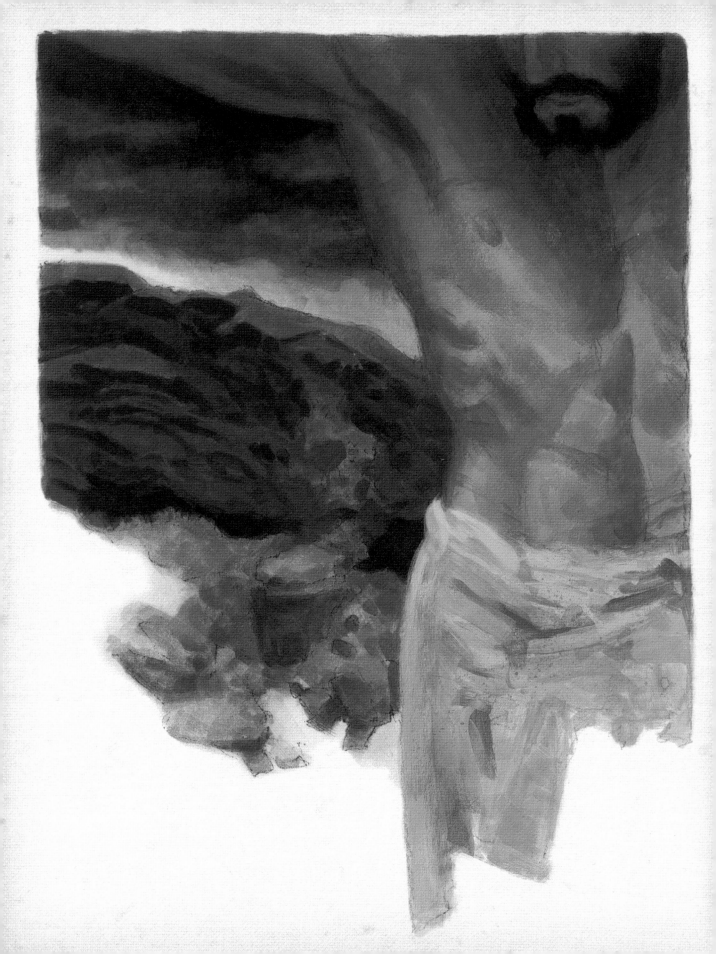

17
Christ Teaches That He Is The Bread Of Life
(Part 2)

In the Middle East of Jesus' day, bread was made from wheat or barley. Many people of the day lived entirely on bread alone! Along with fish, bread was certainly the chief food of Jesus' day.

In shape, it resembled round, flat stones. This fact is important when you are reading the Scriptures. For example, in Matthew 7:9, Christ asked, "Or what man is there of you, whom if his son ask bread, will he give him a stone?" Some people have wondered why Jesus linked bread with a stone in this question. When we see what their bread looked like, however, we can better understand His choice of words. (Someone has said that their bread not only looked like a stone but also was about as hard as one, too!)

The bread was made by mixing the finely beaten wheat with water or milk. It was then kneaded with one's hands in small, wooden bowls called kneading troughs. The bread was then placed in a barrel-shaped hole in the ground that served as an oven. The women baked the bread until it was thoroughly done. Most of the bread was circular, about eight to ten inches in diameter, and one-fourth of an inch thick.

The fact that the boy in John 6 brought barley loaves instead of the more nutritious and delicious wheat bread suggests that he came from a poor family or region. In Judges 7:13, the Midianite's dream of a barley loaf, which was interpreted as the "sword of Gideon," perhaps symbolized the poverty of Israel under the Midianites' oppression.

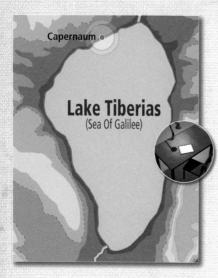

Capernaum

Lake Tiberias
(Sea Of Galilee)

Bread plays a central role in this lesson as it did in the preceding lesson. But as you study this lesson, don't think only in terms of physical bread. Jesus is speaking of spiritual bread. Hopefully you will understand what He meant more clearly than did the Jews!

Student Work

Read John 6:32–71.

If you were part of the crowd, what kind of bread would you have thought Jesus was talking about? _____
_____

- What was the need that you would have wanted to be satisfied?
  _____
  _____

- Was this what Jesus was offering? _____

What do the Jews' complaints in verses 41 and 42 show about their standing with the Father in verses 37–40?_____
_____
_____
_____

How does the drawing work of the Father show its effects in people's lives?_____
_____
_____

What does verse 44 say about who causes and allows us to believe?_____
_____
_____

What do you think it means to eat Jesus' flesh and drink His blood? _____
_____
_____
_____

This photo was taken from the top of the cliffs of Mount Arbel. The north end of the Sea of Galilee can be seen in the distance. Directly below these cliffs is the route that Christ would have taken when traveling between Nazareth and Capernaum.

Unleavened Flatbread

Ingredients
1 cup whole wheat flour
1/4 teaspoon salt
1/4 teaspoon ground cumin or coriander
1/2 cup water, room temperature

Mix flour, salt and cumin or coriander together in a bowl. Slowly work in the water, kneading in a work bowl or on a floured bread board, until the dough is supple and elastic (about 5-10 minutes). Cover with a damp cloth and let rest 30 minutes. Knead again lightly and form into small round balls. Flatten balls with the palm of the hand, lightly flour each side, and place on a board. Roll out thinly.

Heat an ungreased griddle or heaving frying pan on medium heat until a drop of water dances on the surface. Cook one or two flat breads at a time, turning after the bottoms develop brown spots and bread just begins to puff up. Rotate bread gently, while pressing down lightly on the edges. Turn over and lightly brown the other side. When both sides are done, pick up the bread with a fork, and if using a gas burner, hold it for moment over a high flame. This will generally give the bread an extra "push" to puff up. Serve hot.

Note: Often your first attempts might not puff up as well as your third or fourth tries. This generally means that the griddle or frying pan was not sufficiently heated to begin with. These first breads are still delicious! Also, you might want to try adding a tablespoon of butter or samneh to the dough to enrich it. Both varieties are recommended.

Verses 60–66 show that some of Jesus' disciples (not the Twelve) did not like this teaching and abandoned him because they did not believe. What does this say about their commitment to Jesus?

_____

_____

_____

_____

Why didn't Jesus try harder to convince them to follow?

_____

_____

_____

_____

What did Peter understand that the unfaithful disciples did not?

_____

_____

_____

_____

Notes From The Teacher's Lesson

Christ Teaches That He Is The Bread Of Life (Part 2)

The _____ **Bread (6:32–40)**

- Characteristics of the true _____

    - A _____ (vs. 33)

    - Gives _____ (vs. 33)

    - Satisfies (vs. 35)

- Facts about bread

    - A _____

    - Needed daily

    - Must be _____ to be eaten

- Rejection of the true Bread (vs. 34, 36)

The _____ **Bread (6:41–50)**

- Why the _____ rejected Christ (vs. 44–46)

    - Sinful condition

    - Not drawn by the Father

- Impact of the living Bread: those who partake live forever (vs. 47–50)

The _____ **Bread (6:51–59)**

- Refers to Christ's sacrifice on the Cross

- Supplies everlasting life to all who partake in faith

The Results (6:60–71)

- Many people _____ Him (vs. 60–66).

- The _____ stay with Him (vs. 67–71).

    - Only a few are committed enough to remain.

    - The rest seek miracles and food.

Why Men Follow Christ

- Because of the _____ (7:2)

- Because of the _____ (7:5)

- Because of the _____ (6:26)

- Because of the _____ (6:70–71)

- Because He is the _____ (6:68–69)

Digging Deeper

1. Judas followed Jesus for all of the wrong reasons. Conduct a study of the life of Judas, perhaps beginning your research by reading what Lockyer says about him in *All the Men of the Bible*. List the things about Judas that indicate that his heart and motives were not right. What parallels can you make between those characteristics of Judas and modern men? Why did the other eleven disciples not detect Judas' hypocrisy? List characteristics in our or others' lives that could be warning signs that the motives are not right? What steps can we take to correct such characteristics in our own lives or to help those in whom we see such signs?

2. Study the master-servant relationship as explained in Scripture. Explain the difference between the master-servant relationship and the master-slave relationship. What was expected of each person in the master-servant relationship? How does the master-servant relationship correspond to our personal responsibility to Christ? What principles in the master-servant relationship should guide our conduct and behavior as Christians in the workplace? What does the New Testament require of employers and employees?

3. We've all heard the warning "Don't bite the hand that feeds you." How do we see the people to whom Christ fed physical food (albeit miraculously) biting His hand? Why did they turn on Him thus?

4. In His teaching, Christ often used common, everyday things to teach important spiritual truths, just as He used the bread in this lesson. List and describe other common things that He used at other times to teach deep spiritual truths.

18

Christ Attends The Feast Of Tabernacles

Imagine yourself participating in a serious and deeply symbolic formal ceremony that your unique group has performed for centuries. Everything is going as it was planned and as it has been done for generations. Everyone involved takes great pride in doing everything just right, and no one dares to introduce or do anything radical during the event.

Suddenly, someone stands up among the crowd and shouts something that is shockingly radical! In fact, he is making what to many people in attendance are outrageous claims. The leaders of the ceremony would, of course, be very upset with the one who dared to interrupt their ceremony and introduce such an innovation. Spectators and participants alike would be shocked beyond words.

That's just what happened one day during the Jewish ceremony known as the Feast of Tabernacles.

The Feast of Tabernacles was a week-long celebration involving a series of unique customs and ceremonies. For example, at daybreak every morning for the first seven days of the feast, a priest went to the pool of Siloam and filled a golden pitcher with water. He was accompanied by a procession of people and a band playing music.

On returning to the temple, the priest was welcomed by three blasts of a trumpet. Going to the west side of the great altar, he poured the water into

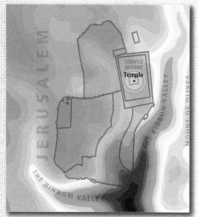

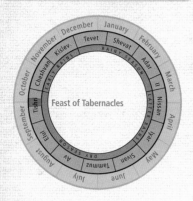

Feast of Tabernacles

a silver basin that had holes in the bottom. The leaking water ran off, and the people sang, shouted, and sounded trumpets.

This interesting ceremony represented three things:

1. The water that God provided for their fathers in the wilderness,
2. The forthcoming "latter rains," (see circle calendar below) and
3. The outpouring of the Holy Spirit at the coming of the Messiah.

On the eighth day of the feast, the ceremony was performed as it had been on the previous seven days, but on this day the water was mixed with wine and poured into two silver cups upon the altar. The people sang from Isaiah 12:3: "with joy shall ye draw water out of the wells of salvation."

When Jesus went to the Feast of Tabernacles, He stood on the eighth day during this very ceremony and cried out, "If any man thirst, let him come unto me, and drink. He that believeth on me, as the Scripture hath said, out of his belly shall flow rivers of living water" (John 7:37–38). Imagine the people's surprise when He interrupted the ceremony! Imagine the frustration and anger of the Jewish rulers when they realized what He was saying about Himself in those words! This incident and the claim that Christ made with those words are the subject of this lesson.

Before we can begin that lesson, however, we must catch up with some things Jesus did that John did not record for us. In His wisdom, however, God inspired the other Gospel writers to record those events for us.

John 6 closes with Jesus in a synagogue in Capernaum in the spring of A.D. 29. John 7 opens with Jesus in Galilee, preparing to go to Jerusalem in September–October A.D. 29. The following table is designed to fill in the historical gap at this point in John's gospel. Read the references in the left column and then complete the table by writing in each of the other two columns where Jesus went and what He did there.

Scripture reference	Where Jesus went	What happened there
Mark 7:24–30		
Mark 7:31–8:9; Matt. 15:29–38		
Mark 8:10–12; Matt. 15:39–16:4		
Mark 8:13–26; Matt. 16:5–12		
Mark 8:27–30; Matt. 16:13–20; Luke 9:18–21		
Mark 9:2–8; Matt. 17:1–8		
Mark 9:30–32; Matt. 17:22–23; Luke 9:43–45		
Matt. 17:24–27		
Matt. 18:1–5; Mark 9:33–37; Luke 9:46–48		
Mark 9:38–50; Matt. 18:6–14; Luke 9:49–50		
Matt. 18:15–35		

After the Babylonians destroyed Solomon's Temple, the Jews under Zerubbabel rebuilt a far less impressive structure in 515 B.C. after their return from captivity. About two decades before Christ's birth, Herod the Great initiated a major expansion and renovation, which was not completed until after his death in 4 B.C. The structure in Jesus time was known as Herod's Temple.

About 30 years after Jesus' death, the Jews rebelled against the Roman occupying forces. Roman legions lay siege to Jerusalem and razed Herod's Temple in A.D. 70. Seen here is the retaining wall, which is the only remaining portion of the original structure. It is known today as the western, or "Wailing Wall." Orthodox Jews hold the site sacred today, offering prayers for the restoration of the temple and Old Testament worship.

Student Work

Read John 7:1–31.

Why would Jesus' brothers want Him to show Himself to everyone when even they did not believe in Him? _____
_____
_____
_____

Some of the Jews thought Jesus was a deceiver. What kind of deception were they talking about? What might they have thought was the lie Jesus was perpetrating? _____
_____
_____
_____
_____

The Jews were surprised at Jesus' knowledge because he had not sat under the teaching of their rabbis. What was the source of Jesus' teaching? _____
_____
_____
_____

What does the rabbis' question suggest about where they were looking for their authority?_____
_____
_____
_____

What does verse 17 teach is the determining factor in allowing us to understand the source of Jesus' authority? _____
_____
_____
_____

What is suggested by the fact that the Jews wanted to seize Jesus? Did they think he was a lunatic or someone blaspheming by claiming to be God? _____
_____
_____

What does verse 31 show that Jesus' miracles had accomplished in some people's hearts? _____
_____
_____
_____

Notes From The Teacher's Lesson

Christ Attends The Feast Of Tabernacles

Reasons For Christ's Absence From The Public Spotlight

- _____ temperatures
- Pharisees are growing more _____ .
- People are excited about making Him _____ .
- Herod is growing _____ .
- Christ needs _____ .
- Christ needs time to _____ His brothers.

His Brothers' Selfish Request (7:1–5)

- Urge Jesus to attend the feast
- Fail to understand about His impending death

Jesus' Reasons For Not Going To The Feast (7:6–9)

- Not His _____ (vs. 6)
- Not His purpose to _____ (vs. 7–8)

Jesus Goes To The Feast In Secret (7:10–13)

Results Of Jesus' Teaching In The Temple (7:14–31)

- People marvel at His _____ (vs. 15–16).
- Christ accuses the people of seeking to kill Him (vs. 19).
- People _____ that they would kill Him (vs. 20).
- Christ exposes their ignorance (vs. 21–24).
- People become even more confused (vs. 25–27).
- Jesus claims to _____ (vs. 28–29).
- Jews seek to kill Him (vs. 30).
- Many Believe on Him (7:31)

The Feast of Tabernacles was initiated to commemorate the 40 years in the wilderness when Israel lived in temporary dwellings. Many people built small tents, or "booths," and lived in them during this feast. This map shows the route followed by the priests and a procession of the people as they carried water from the Pool of Siloam to pour out on the altar at the temple.

On the last day of the feast all the pilgrims in the city joined the procession with the priests. They divided into three groups. One remained at the temple for the morning sacrifices. A second group left the city through the East Gate to cut willow branches to place on the sacrificial altar. The remaining group followed the water priest to the Pool of Siloam, where he filled a golden pitcher with water. The procession then returned to the temple through the Water Gate, led by the priest.

Digging Deeper

1. Read Leviticus 23:34–44 concerning the regulations for the Feast of Tabernacles, and answer the following questions. What was the date of the event? How long did the feast last? What customs were followed during the feast and why?

2. Read about and report to the class on significance of the Feast of Tabernacles as described in chapter 5 (pp. 45–55) of Buksbazen's book *The Gospel in the Feasts of Israel*.

3. Is Satan concerned about the influence that your life has over the other people around you? What practical steps can you take in each of the following environments to ensure that your life is having the type of influence it ought?

   • Your home
   • Your extended family (i.e., grandparents, aunts, uncles, cousins, etc.)
   • Your church youth group
   • Your school classroom
   • Your extracurricular activities
   • Your community and neighborhood

19

Christ Divides The People At The Feast Of Tabernacles

Lisa is a medical missionary to Bangladesh. She knows that winning converts is hard there because the society is so much different than it is here in the United States. Yet she is committed to bringing Bangladeshis to a decision either for or against Christ while she's trying to meet their medical needs.

Bangladesh is about the size of the state of Tennessee, but whereas Tennessee has a population of about eleven million people, Bangladesh is crammed with about 132 million people! According to the *World Factbook* of the U. S. Central Intelligence Agency (CIA), Bangladesh is "one of the world's poorest, most densely populated, and least developed nations." More than two-thirds of its workers are employed in agriculture, but the unemployment rate there is 35 percent. The agricultural production is regularly hindered alternately by severe drought and cyclones and flooding. The per capita annual income is only $1,570, less than most of your parents make in a month, or perhaps even a week. Only slightly more than half of the people over the age of fifteen can read and write.

Eighty-three percent of Bangladeshis are Muslim. Sixteen percent are Hindu. The remaining one percent are either animists, believers in some obscure tribal religions, or Christian in the broadest sense of the term,

which includes Roman Catholics, Jehovah's Witnesses, Mormons, etc. Very few Bangladeshis are true believers because the society makes believers pay a very high price for their profession of faith.

For example, Lisa relates how a Bangladeshi man who gets saved might have his rice paddies destroyed by his neighbors, thereby devastating him economically because that is his livelihood. After all, the primary money crop of the nation is rice production. If he has a little vegetable stand or rug-selling business in the local market, other Bangladeshis will no longer do business with him. He might even be attacked and beaten to death.

Bangladeshi women who become true Christians have an even harder time. According to the Bangladeshi customs, when a woman marries, she leaves her own family for good and goes to live with her husband in his parents' house. If she gets saved, she is kicked out of the house and has neither a legitimate means of earning a living (women in Bangladesh are not educated, so they cannot conduct a business) nor anywhere to live. She becomes destitute. She gets no support from her husband or his family; as far as they are concerned, she is dead, and her husband will easily find another wife.

The mission agency of which Lisa is a part established a special ministry called "Heart House" to take care of such women. There they learn special craft skills so that they can earn a living, purchase food, and provide for any children that they might have. One elderly Christian woman raised five children through the work that she did in "Heart House."

For these reasons, if a Bangladeshi decides to accept Christ, he or she faces a severe reality: living for Christ costs them a great price. How unlike America, where, by contrast, living for Christ seems to carry hardly any price at all! How ashamed we believers should be whenever we are afraid to take a public stand for Christ or witness for Him.

As you study this lesson about how Christ divided the people, ask yourself how you would have responded if you had been there at the Feast of Tabernacles and heard Christ's call to decision. How are you responding to His call today?

Student Work

Read John 7:32–53.

The Pharisees obviously disagreed with Jesus' teaching, but people don't usually try to arrest those they disagree with. If you were one of these Pharisees, why would you have wanted to go after Him?

_____

_____

_____

_____

When Jesus said He would go somewhere, the Jews thought that Jesus was going leave them to teach Gentiles who had begun to follow Judaism. Why didn't they understand what Jesus was saying? _____

_____

_____

_____

Imagine that you were a Jew in Jesus' day. What might have made you want to side with the Pharisees against Jesus? _____

_____

_____

_____

What does it seem to you that the Jewish people wanted Jesus to be? _____

_____

Would you have wanted what they wanted? Why or why not?

_____

_____

_____

_____

What do you think the officers meant by their response to the chief priests and Pharisees in verse 46? _____

_____

_____

Was this a valid excuse for their disobedience? _____

Scripture doesn't tell us if Nicodemus ever believed in Jesus. If he was a believer, do you think he was bold enough before the Pharisees? Why or why not? _____

_____

_____

_____

What would you have done in his place? _____

_____

_____

_____

Notes From The Teacher's Lesson

Christ Divides The People At The Feast Of Tabernacles

Jesus Is _____ *(7:32–36).*

Jesus Cries Out To The _____ *(7:37–39).*

- The Jewish ceremony

- Jesus' meaning

The People Are _____ *(7:40–53).*

- Some believe He is the _____ (vs. 40–41).

- Some remain _____ (vs. 41–42).

- Some _____ Him (vs. 44).

- Some are _____ (vs. 45–49).

- One _____ Him (vs. 50–53).

Digging Deeper

1. Explain what it is about the gospel message that divides people. Why does it cause such division? Why does an active, obedient Christianity run contrary to the political correctness of "tolerance" for all religious views?

The East Gate of Jerusalem as seen from the Kidron Valley. This gate was built by the Turks over the site of the gate that existed in Christ's day.

2. Read and study Joshua 24:15 carefully. In this verse, Joshua forced the people to make a clear choice. Name some instances in which you have been called upon to make a clear-cut decision in a matter that put your Christianity to the test. Explain how you made the decision(s) and describe the results.

3. Describe the times when you've made a public statement of a spiritual decision. What benefits did you discover in such a public announcement? Did it lead to suffering or persecution of any kind? If so, how?

4. Contact a mission agency and gather information about a particular country where the agency has a missionary. Write to the missionary and ask about the price that the people there must pay (socially, financially, physically, etc.) whenever they confess Christ publicly. Ask what you can do to help those people. Then do it!

Unit 5

Christ's Public Ministry Prompts Mixed Reactions

20
The Day After The Feast

Who was the most profound writer in the Bible?

Did you say the apostle Paul? That might be a good guess. He wrote a lot of deep theological stuff. But he also wrote some of the most practical, down-to-earth books in the Bible. But the answer is not Paul.

Did someone else say David? Yes, David certainly wrote some beautiful psalms. In fact, David wrote the longest book in the Bible—Psalms. But David isn't the answer either.

Perhaps it was Moses? After all, Moses received the Ten Commandments directly from God's hand. No, the answer isn't Moses.

Oh, so you think that perhaps it was Solomon, the wisest man? He did speak great words of wisdom. In fact, some of his proverbs are much deeper in meaning and significance than one might think from a mere cursory reading of the books of Proverbs and Ecclesiastes. But not even Solomon qualifies to be called the most profound writer in the Bible.

That distinction belongs to someone we don't usually think of as being a writer at all—Jesus Christ!

Yes, Jesus wrote, but what He wrote didn't even survive for a day. We certainly don't have a copy of His writing today. In fact, the Bible doesn't even record what He wrote—and yet it was profoundly powerful.

Read John 8:1–11. This passage tells us that Christ indeed wrote something on the ground, but it doesn't say what He wrote. Some Bible

scholars have suggested that he wrote the names of the accusing Pharisees who were around Him that day—and listed each of their sins! (They base their view on Jeremiah 17:13: "…they that depart from me shall be written in the earth, because they have forsaken the Lord, the fountain of living waters.")

We don't know this, of course, but if that is indeed what He wrote, we can understand why the Pharisees reacted the way they did—they quietly left the area! That was profound and effective writing.

Regardless of *what* Christ wrote, we know what the *effects* were, and we can learn several lessons from this account. Commentator Matthew Henry probably said it best when he wrote, "It is impossible to tell…what He wrote; but this is the only mention made in the gospels of Christ's writing. Christ by this teaches us to be slow to speak when difficult cases are proposed to us, not quick to "shoot our bolt." Think twice before we speak once. But, when Christ seemed as though He heard them not, He made it appear that He not only heard their words, but knew their thoughts."

Look for other lessons that this incident teaches us as you read, study, and listen to the teacher's lesson.

 ## Student Work

Read John 8:1–59.

What would you have thought about Jesus if you were the adulterous woman brought before Him? _____

_____

_____

Jesus says He is "the light." What does this imply about some people's belief that there are many ways to God and eternal life?

_____

_____

_____

When the Jews asked where Jesus' father was, what were they implying about his family background? _____

_____

_____

Have you ever tried to discredit someone by bringing up rumors about them? Pause and think about your answer.

What does it mean to abide in Jesus' word? _____
_____
_____

What would you say to a person who claimed to be a Christian, but is not abiding in His word?_____
_____

Committing sin in verse 34 refers to a habit of sinning as a pattern of life. What does Jesus say he offers to His sons? _____
_____

What would you have thought of Jesus if He told you your father was the devil? Would you have been convicted in your heart, or would you have wanted to attack Him? _____
_____
_____
_____

What did Jesus mean when He said, "Before Abraham was, I am"?
_____
_____
_____

What would you have thought if you saw a man claiming to be older than a man who died hundreds of years before?_____
_____
_____
_____

Why did the Jews try to stone Him? Why were they so angry at what He said?_____
_____
_____
_____

Do you think verse 59 describes a miracle? Why or why not?
_____
_____
_____
_____

Stoning

Rabbis recorded ancient traditions of law enforcement in the Mishnah. There, they explain that stoning was not carried out by throwing stones at the person until death, which is the common understanding. Rather, the convicted criminal was pushed off a two-story platform, and then stones were dropped on him. The first witness was the one who pushed him off, and if he died the process was complete. If the person was still alive, then the second witness threw a large stone on him. If he was still alive, then the rest of the crowd threw stones at him. The Rabbis forbade further disfiguration of the body. Witnesses were required to take part in the stoning, ensuring that they believed their testimony firmly enough to actually carry out the execution themselves. In some cases this would certainly discourage false testimony.

Notes From The Teacher's Lesson

The Day After The Feast

The Wisdom Of Christ (8:1–11)

- The _____ (vs. 3–6)

- The _____ (vs. 6–8)

  - Shows Respect to the _____

  - Shows the _____ of the Leaders

- The _____ (vs. 9)

The Ignorance Of The Pharisees (8:13–52)

- Ignorance of His _____ (vs. 13)

- Ignorance of His _____ (vs. 19)

- Ignorance of His _____ (vs. 22)

- Ignorance of His _____ (vs. 25)

- Ignorance of their own _____ (vs. 33)

- Ignorance of His _____ (vs. 48)

- Ignorance of His _____ (vs. 53)

- Ignorance of His _____ (vs. 57)

The Outcome Of Their Ignorance

Digging Deeper

1. According to 1 Corinthians 2:14, the "natural man" cannot understand the truths of God because they seem to him to be "foolishness." Why is this true? Give examples of instances that prove the spiritual ignorance of the unbeliever. First Corinthians 2:15, however, says that "he that is spiritual" can understand the truths of God. What is the difference that makes such understanding possible for the believer? Give examples of instances that prove the believer's ability to discern spiritual truth. List steps that believers can take to increase their spiritual discernment and understanding.

2. Read carefully Matthew 5:43–48, which deals with the way we are to treat others. Why is the application of this passage so difficult for us? According to these verses, how are we to treat our enemies, those who hate or despise us, mistreat us, speak evil of us, or accuse us falsely? Have you been a victim of such mistreatment? How did you respond? If your response did not conform to the principles of Matthew 5:43–48, what steps can you take now to correct your improper conduct toward that person? Now do it!

3. Define truth in scriptural terms. What is the foundation of a scriptural definition of truth? How does today's relativistic society define truth? Why are these two definitions in such conflict? Give examples of how the relativistic definition of truth is evident in society today. What effect does one's definition of truth have on his or her everyday attitudes and actions? List steps that you can take daily that will ensure that you live your life in accordance with the scriptural definition of truth?

4. In John 8:56, Jesus said, "Abraham rejoiced to see my day." Explain how Abraham saw Christ's day when hundreds of years separated the two. (Use Scripture to support your explanation.)

5. Write an essay explaining how a believer should and should not address or deal with sin in the lives of others? Include Scripture references and give both Bible examples and everyday modern instances to support each of your points.

21
The Man Born Blind

The Bible—and life, for that matter—is filled with paradoxes. (A paradox is a statement that seems to contradict common sense but is nonetheless true.) For example, the Bible says that it's better to give than to receive; that one who saves his life will lose it, but one who loses his life for Christ's sake will find it; and that we serve ourselves best when we serve others. Common sense tells us that to follow such paradoxes is a sure-fire road to failure!

The world's philosophy, on the other hand, tells us just the opposite: get all you can and give only what you must; put yourself and your own needs and desires first. Do whatever it takes, regardless of what it does to others, to achieve your goals. After all, it's a dog-eat-dog world out there, and you have to learn to swim with the sharks—and bite back if necessary!

In spite of the number of seemingly successful people who have followed the world's philosophy of success, those people are not really successful at all. When they lose all of the outward trappings of their "success," they have nothing left. Some people, however, refuse to buy in to that self-destructive philosophy, preferring to follow the paradoxical principles of Scripture in their quest for *true* success.

Take, for example, the late Mary Kay Ashe, founder of the famous Mary Kay Cosmetics company. (Perhaps some of your mothers even sell for that company!) Her philosophy was based on what she called "Golden Rule Management." She treated people—both her customers and her employees—the way she wanted other people to treat her. To her, people

came first. "To me," she wrote in her book *Mary Kay on People Management*, *P* and *L* doesn't only mean profit and loss—it also means *people and love.*"

According to Mary Kay, you gain success by building people up, praising their accomplishments and improvements, making them feel important, listening to them, and helping them become successful. In the process, you also become successful. This is what Denis Waitley calls "the double win." The people whom you help win, and *you* win, too!

Business trends writer John Naisbitt wrote, "Mary Kay's common sense guide to the new people-centered management is a wonderful, high-touch antidote to all those boring business school books." But in a sense, Naisbitt was only partially right. He was wrong in thinking that Mary Kay's ideas were new. In reality, they are as old as the Bible!

If you will follow the principles of God's Word—especially the seeming paradoxes—you, too, will find that success, satisfaction, and true joy comes from putting others before yourself. It's quaint but true that you spell *joy* like this: Jesus first, Others second, and Yourself last. As you study this lesson on the life of Christ, notice how He lived and taught this very principle. Then put it into practice in your own life and see just how true it is!

Student Work

Read John 9:1–41.

Jesus said that a man was born blind so that God's power might be shown through him. Explain an obstacle in your life or in your family that may exist so God can show you His power._____

_____

_____

_____

If you were a Pharisee, why would you be so angry that a man was healed? Would you be primarily concerned about the Sabbath, or would you have another motivation for your anger?_____

_____

_____

_____

_____

During Hezekiah's fortification of Jerusalem, he built a tunnel system for moving water from a spring east of the city walls into several pools or cisterns inside the city. One of these, the Pool of Siloam, was used not only for a civil water supply, but also as part of the memorial ceremony for the Feast of Tabernacles.

New Testament Diseases

Category	Symptoms	Cause	Reference
Paralysis	Loss of muscle control, often beginning with extremities; sometimes progressive and resulting in death; sometimes leading to physical deformity	Variety of possible causes depending on specific malady, including infection, injury, and genetic defect	Matthew 8, 9, 12; Mark 2, 3; Luke 5, 6, 7; John 5; Acts 3, 9, 14
Blindness	Complete or partial loss of sight	Most often genetic defect or childhood illness	Matthew 20; Mark 7, 8, 10; John 9
Skin diseases	Often refers to leprosy, which in Scripture includes a variety of diseases; symptoms include skin discoloration, nerve damage, open sores, loss of appendages, etc. Other less serious diseases were also present, including vitiligo, which is the loss of skin pigment.	Most often bacterial infections	Matthew 8, 10, 26; Mark 1; Luke 5, 17
Bowel diseases	Fever, intestinal obstruction, severe infection	Herod Agrippa's disease was likely related to a fly and maggot infestation of his body; Publius' father may have suffered from malaria or cholera	Acts 12, 28
Dropsy	Abnormal accumulation of watery fluid in body cavities or tissues	Uncertain, perhaps a nerve condition that causes blood vessels to malfunction	Luke 14
Hemorrhage	Unstoppable bleeding, leading to deteriorating physical condition	Uncertain	Matthew 9; Mark 5; Luke 8
Epilepsy	Involuntary seizures, sudden loss of body control	Connected in several passages to demon possession; apparently not always identical to modern epilepsy	Matthew 4, 17; Mark 9; Luke 9

Do you think the blind man's parents took the easy way out because of their fear? _____

What would you have done differently? _____

_____

_____

_____

Irony is a situation that is opposite from what we might expect. This chapter shows a tremendous irony about who is blind to the truth about Christ and who can see it. How is irony present in this chapter? Look closely at verses 30–34 and 39–41. _____

_____

_____

_____

_____

In this chapter and others before, the Pharisees are constantly attacking Jesus because of their spiritual blindness. Do you think they know the truth about him but are intentionally rejecting it, or are they so stuck in their tradition that they don't understand? Why do you think so? _____

_____

_____

_____

_____

_____

Notes From The Teacher's Lesson

The Man Born Blind

The _____ *Of The Savior (9:1)*

- Christ is never too busy to win someone to Himself.

- Christ is more concerned with the welfare of others than His own.

- Christ notices the outcasts of our society whom the typical person shuns.

The _____ *Of The Disciples (9:2–5)*

- Their _____ : physical problems are _____ for sin.

- The _____ : physical ailments allow God to manifest His _____ .

  - Fanny Crosby

  - Paul Hutchins

  - Ron Hamilton

The _____ *Of The Miracle (9:6–7)*

The _____ *Of The Blind Man (9:8–34)*

- Sight first, then salvation

- Progressive sight

  - A man called Jesus (vs. 11)

  - A prophet (vs. 17)

  - Of God (vs. 30–33)

- The Pool of Siloam

The _____ *of the Blind Man (9:35–38)*

- Washes in the water

- Begins to see

- Confesses Jesus as Lord and believes

- Worships His Lord

 Digging Deeper

1. The world's philosophy is "Look out for Number One—yourself!" In reality, however, the greatest success (in fact, the only true success) comes when we put others before ourselves and try to meet their needs. Explain how this attitude of helping meet the needs of others and putting others before ourselves can be applied in (a) family, (b) sports, (c) business, and (d) ministry.

2. Study the life of John Wannamaker to learn about the biblical principles that he applied to his successful business. Alternatively, study the life of J. C. Penney, the founder of what became known during his lifetime as "the Golden Rule Store," and explain how it got that reputation.

3. List specific things that you can do to help meet the needs of others in your community and thereby show them that you truly care about them. What can we do as (a) individuals, (b) a church, (c) a youth group, (d) a school?

4. Many schools and other organizations often raise money for worthy community causes by staging a "walk-a-thon." Identify a particular community need and then organize your own class, school, club, or youth group in a similar activity with a different twist—stage a "work-a-thon!" Instead of mere walking a specified distance in return for contributions, offer to work for the contributions to the cause. Pick up litter along a certain stretch of highway, rake the leaves or mow the lawns of senior citizens, clean windows for invalids, etc. Show the community that you care by doing something worthwhile—even if they contribute nothing!

5. Write an essay giving a scriptural reason for why "bad" things sometimes happen to "good" people. Use Scripture and real-life examples to illustrate and support your points.

6. Conduct a study of the life of Job. Focus especially on his reactions to the "bad" things that happened to him. When "bad" things happen to us, why shouldn't we complain or try to escape the problems? What should we do instead? What lessons can we learn and apply from such adversity that will strengthen our faith in God and be a witness and testimony to others around us?

7. Typical of today's ethics is the idea that if someone is experiencing dire, possibly life-threatening, health problems, they have a "right to die" because they can no longer have the "quality of life" that allows them to live in "dignity." Such a philosophy encourages suicide, physician-assisted suicide, and euthanasia ("mercy killing"). Refute the "quality of life" argument, giving Scripture as supporting evidence.

8. Explain and illustrate Cotton Mather's statement, "What can't be cured can be endured."

9. Read and report on a biography of Fanny Crosby. Explain how she allowed her adversity to bless others rather than create a bad spirit within her. What lessons from her life can people with disabilities learn?

10. Read and report on one of the books on the Recommended Reading List by Dave Dravecky or Dennis Byrd. Explain that person's adversity, how he overcame it, and what he learned from it.

11. Read the following and report on the difficulty of trusting Christ in the first century. Include your thoughts on a) how difficult it would be for you to have trusted Christ had you lived then; b) the effect the church would feel today if it was as difficult for a person to claim to be saved; c) how Jewish treatment of the disobedient differs from Christ's directives on church discipline (Matt. 18:15–17).

> Excommunication in Christ's day:
>
> According to the Talmud, there were three grades of excommunication in Judaism. The first was called Nidden, and those on whom it was pronounced were forbidden for thirty days to have any communication with any person except at a distance of six feet! They could not attend worship services during the thirty days and could not shave during that time. They also were required to wear garments of mourning. The second was called Cherem, and was pronounced on those who were still not repentant after the first excommunication. The offender was officially cursed and not allowed to talk with anyone or to enter the temple for any reason. The third, Shammatha, was inflicted on those who were still unrepentant after Cherem. They were cut off from all connection with Jewish society and were cursed to utter destruction.
>
> There were two basic reasons for excommunication: refusing to pay money required by law, and despising the Word of God or the word of the scribes. The blind man faced excommunication because of his belief in Jesus Christ as the Messiah (9:22, 34). In John 12:42, 43 some would not confess Christ publicly for fear of excommunication. Notice what Jesus predicted in John 16:2, 3.

22

The Good Shepherd Message

As these words are being written, our nation is at war. We are at war with a unique enemy, an enemy that does not use conventional armies, navies, or air forces. It is an enemy that is seldom seen or, if seen, recognized as the enemy. It is an enemy that plans its attacks secretly, using against us the very freedoms that they would take from us. It is a ruthless enemy that will attack and kill innocent civilians, including women and children, as readily as a conventional enemy would attack a military base. It is an enemy that is so fanatical that its soldiers are willing to commit suicide in ways that kill and maim many innocent people and wreak terror among us—because they believe that by doing so they will become martyrs and enter Paradise immediately upon their death.

This enemy is Islamic terrorism. It knows no borders. It follows no rules of conventional warfare. And it is the end product of a false religion. But this enemy is not a new, twenty-first-century phenomenon. It's as old as Islam itself. It is the same product of Islam that threatened to take over Europe in the late seventh century. Having easily conquered Syria and Egypt, the Muslims (then called Moors) raced across North Africa, invaded Spain, and looked greedily northward toward the kingdom of the Franks (modern France), which was on the east regularly threatened by the Slavs and internally torn by bickering nobles and a disunited and decaying society.

Taking advantage of the disarray of the Franks, the Moors swept into France with their swift and deadly cavalry, an innovation in warfare. Their

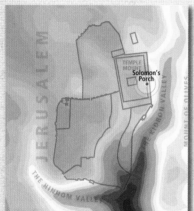

mission was to conquer the world for Islam in order to make their religion the world religion—even if they had to kill all infidels who stood in their way. Their success seemed assured by their swift and brutal attack.

By God's grace, however, one ruler dared to fight them to the end. Charles Martel, the mayor of the city of Tours in central France, got the nobles back in line, unified the divided people, strengthened the kingdom against the Slavs, and began to "put the medieval knight on horseback."

Then, in 732, Martel met the Moors in battle at Tours and defeated them badly. They retreated toward Spain under cover of darkness, never to return again. Until now. But now they are returning not as a massive invading army but as "sleeper cells" of terrorists who are trained to blend in as "normal people" among the citizenry—until they receive a secret signal to launch their random attacks against "the infidel."

What makes this enemy so difficult to defeat is that our society is a free society in which anyone can believe basically anything. Our society, like that of the Franks before the rise of Charles "The Hammer" Martel, is in moral decay. We are continually being told that we must value all religious views equally and that to promote our own view of Christianity is to be intolerant. We are told that "all religions lead to heaven," "we all worship the same God, just by different names," and other slogans of "tolerance."

The problem is that all of that is untrue. The Bible, the source of all truth—especially spiritual truth—says that all religions are *not* equal. There is only *one* way to heaven. There is only *one* God, and whoever worships anyone other than that one true God is a deceiver and a liar. Jesus Christ said, "*I* am *the* way, *the* truth, and *the* life. No man cometh unto the Father but by *me*." That's pretty limiting. That's exclusive. That's intolerant. But it's the truth.

Yes, our nation is at war against terrorism. But every Christian has *always* been at war with the powers of darkness from the moment of his or her salvation. Even in Jesus' day false Messiahs were commonplace, and He Himself prophesied of many more to come. Counterfeit's to truth are nothing new. As you study this lesson, consider the difference between what other religions have to offer and what Christ offers. How does Jesus' promise of provision and sustenance differ from way of salvation false religions proclaim?

Student Work

Read John 9:39–10:21.

What did a first century shepherd do for his sheep that Jesus does for His flock of believers? _____

_____

_____

Since Jesus was talking to Jews, who might be the "other sheep" of verse 16?_____

_____

_____

What kind of person is the servant described in verses 13–14? _____

_____

Why is he not as dedicated to the safety of the sheep? _____

_____

_____

First century shepherds used different kinds of enclosures for their flocks depending on the terrain and whether they were able to stay in one place for an extended time. Shepherds used caves where they were available and built thorn bush walls when they were on the move. More permanent sheepfolds were built with stone walls, and some had roofs to keep out the weather. All three of these enclosures had one characteristic in common—just one entrance. One of the shepherds would sleep in this doorway in order to protect the flock from predators who might try to enter during the night.

🖊 Imagine that you are a sheep with a high enough "sheep IQ" to understand all that the shepherd does for you. How would you feel toward the shepherd? _____
_____
_____

🖊 How faithful are you to stop and have those same feelings about your Savior? _____
_____
_____

📖 Notes From The Teacher's Lesson

The Good Shepherd Message

Blind _____ **(9:39–41)**

Thieves And _____ **(10:1)**

- The sheepfold
  - Place of _____
  - Physical description
- Definition of a thief
  - One who breaks into a house to steal
  - Usually enters somewhere other than the door
  - Applied to Eastern religions
    - Buddhists: seek nirvana, or extinction of desire
    - Hindus: seek nirvana, believing it is the ultimate reunion with Brahman
    - Muslims: seek a paradise of wine, women, and song

The _____ **Sheep (10:2–6)**

- Hear the _____ of the Shepherd (vs. 4)
- Will not follow a _____ (vs. 6)

The _____ **(10:7–13)**

- Those who were _____ to watch the sheep
- Chief concern was their personal _____ , not the welfare of the sheep

The _____ **Shepherd (10:14–18)**

- Predicts His own _____

- His life is _____, not taken.

Digging Deeper

1. Conduct a detailed study of one of the following religions: Buddhism, Hinduism, Islam, Unification Church, or one of the various cults. Describe its major beliefs and explain how they are unscriptural, especially concerning the doctrine of Christ (2 John 9–11).

2. Read and summarize Walter Martin's book *The Kingdom of the Cults*. What questions in your mind does he address effectively or ineffectively?

3. Read *Islam: An Introduction for Christians* (Paul Varo Martinson, ed.) to gain greater insight into the beliefs and dangers of Islam today.

4. For a shocking report of the inroads of "foreign religions" into our "Christian" society, read *Alien Gods on American Turf* by Terry Muck.

5. Study the fold-out chart titled *The Spirit of Truth and the Spirit of Error* by Keith L. Brooks. Prepare a presentation to explain the chart to your class.

6. Why do cults and false religions thrive today? What aspects of modern American society encourage the growth and proliferation of cults and false religions?

7. What is the best antidote against being infected with the heretical teachings of cults and false religions? What steps are you taking to inoculate yourself against such false teachings?

8. Study the history of the Crusades. Why were the Crusades inconsistent with biblical Christianity? What are the ongoing effects of the Crusades upon Muslim-Christian relations?

9. Write a paper illustrating the futility of our nation's trying to accept all religions as equally valid and truthful.

23
The Feast Of Dedication

"Merry Christmas!"

"Feliz navidad!"

"Noel!"

"He's the reason for the season!"

"Peace on earth, good will toward men!"

"Happy Hanukkah!"

What? you might be wondering. *Happy Hanukkah? What's* that *doing among all of those other Christmas-related sayings?*

While we are celebrating Christmas, the birth of Christ, the incarnation and virgin birth, Jews are celebrating their own holiday called Hanukkah. Some people think that the Jews just invented the holiday to offset the Christians' emphasis on the birth of Christ, whom the Jews rejected. But did you know that Hanukkah was even celebrated during the time of Jesus' ministry?

What we now hear referred to as Hanukkah was originally called the Feast of Dedication, or the Festival of Lights, and it recalls historical events that occurred before the time of Christ.

In about 168 B.C., a Greek ruler named Antiochus IV Epiphanes, in retreating before the Roman legions in Egypt, settled for a time in Jerusalem and began to introduce aspects of the Greek culture among the Jews. According to *Eerdmans Dictionary of the Bible*, he "decreed new laws in place of the Torah [Jewish sacred writings and oral traditions], and

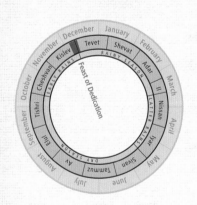

brought a new order of worship to the Jerusalem temple." Jewish historians called what Antiochus Epiphanes did to the temple "desolating sacrilege." Daniel of the Bible called it the "abomination of desolation" (Dan. 11:31; 12:11), as did Jesus (Matt. 24:15; Mark 13:14). He essentially turned the temple into a place of pagan worship and thereby desecrated or polluted everything that the Jews held sacred.

Led by a man named Judas the Maccabee (Maccabeus), the Jews rose up and revolted against Antiochus, establishing their own dynasty of rulers known as the Hasmoneans, or the Maccabees. One of the first acts of Judas Maccabeus after the overthrow of the Greeks was to purify and restore the temple and consecrate a new altar so that Jews could once again worship there. According to Jewish historian Josephus, Judas Maccabeus then threw a big celebration for the people:

"[H]e feasted them upon very rich and splendid sacrifices; and he honoured God, and delighted them, by hymns and psalms. Nay, they were so very glad at the revival of their customs, when after a long time of intermission, they unexpectedly had regained the freedom of their worship, that they made it law for their posterity, that they should keep a festival, on account of the restoration of their temple worship, for eight days. And from that time to this we celebrate this festival, and call it Lights."

Throughout the years afterward, the Jews remembered that event by celebrating the Feast of Dedication, or the Festival of Lights. One tradition that the Jewish celebrants established was that of lighting their houses during this special holiday.

This same celebration was later called by the Hebrew word for "light"—*Hanukkah*. The celebration today tends to focus on a Talmudic tradition which says that "a small amount of oil, found by the Maccabees upon their recovery of the temple…miraculously burned for eight days."

This Jewish holiday occurs during the Jewish month Kislev (our December) and roughly corresponds to our Christmas season. This is the very feast that was being celebrated when Christ was in Jerusalem in John 10:22: "And it was at Jerusalem the feast of the dedication, and it was winter."

Before we begin the study of this lesson in the life of Christ, however, we must once again "fill in the gap" that John leaves in the life of Christ between John 10:21 and 10:22. (According to Luke, a lot happened in that tiny gap between those two verses!) As you did in earlier lessons, read the references in the following table and tell what happened in each reference.

Scripture reference	What happened
Luke 10:1–24	
Luke 10:25–37	
Luke 10:38–42	
Luke 11:1–13	
Luke 11:14–36	
Luke 11:37–54	
Luke 12:1–59	Jesus told three parables:
• vs. 16–21	
• vs. 37–40	
• vs. 42–48	
Luke 13:10–21	

Student Work

Read John 10:22–39.

 Is the question in verse 24 a reasonable question? Had Jesus given any reason for them to be in doubt? _____

_____

What does Jesus imply was the reason for his signs and works?

_____

_____

_____

We've mentioned before that some people believe that Jesus never claimed to be God. What evidence in this passage proves that those people are wrong? _____

_____

_____

_____

Notes From The Teacher's Lesson

The Feast Of Dedication

Christ's Ministry In The Fall Of A.D. 31

- Returns to _____

- Teaches the disciples

- Sends out 70 disciples

- Works southward through _____

The Feast Of Dedication

- Instituted in 164 B.C. by Judas Maccabeus

- Also known as the Festival of _____

- Today known as _____

The Message From Solomon's Porch (10:25–39)

- His _____

  - His _____ prove His deity (vs. 25)

    - His message is matchless (John 3:16).

  - His _____ prove His deity (vs. 25, 38)

- His _____

  - Power to save and to keep (vs. 28–29)

  - The Father's _____ (vs. 30–33)

  - Bold and _____ (vs. 32)

  - Wise and _____ (vs. 34–39)

  - Sent by God the Father (vs. 36)

  - The Father's Son (vs. 36)

Lesson For Our lives

- We should give our lives to know Christ and His Word.

- Evil men will never achieve final triumph over Christ

Digging Deeper

1. Conduct a more detailed study of the historical background of the Jewish holiday of Hanukkah. Explain how it is celebrated in the Jewish community today. (Perhaps interview a Jewish family to get an explanation of specific special things they do during this season.)

2. Research and report on the life and activity of either Judas Maccabeus or Antiochus Epiphanes. (A good beginning source of information might be the writings of Jewish historian Josephus.)

3. Analyze and study 1 Peter 3:15. Break the verse into logical sections and explain the lessons that each phrase holds for believers. What steps must we take to fulfill this command?

24
Christ Ministers In Perea And Bethany

You're doing everything you're supposed to be doing. You've followed all of the rules. You've tried your best to determine God's will and are trying to follow it faithfully and obediently. And then, just when you think you're on the right track and cruising along accomplishing your best for God—BANG!

Everything suddenly seems to go wrong. People disappoint you or betray your trust. Best friends suddenly turn into worst enemies. The best-laid plans fail, or something tragic happens to prevent you from following the pathway you thought God wanted you to go. Money dries up. Worst of all, God doesn't even seem to hear your prayers.

"Lord, why?" you might ask. Or, "Why *me*, Lord?" Before long, if you're not careful, you're doubting God and are ready to give up.

Ever been there? No? Then just wait, because you will be sooner or later. That's life.

Perhaps one of the best Bible examples of that reality is Joseph. He was the "good boy" in his family, doing all of the right things at the right time, and he was his father's favorite. In fact, his father even gave him a unique and special garment. He even had sweet dreams. Everything was going well for him—until he told his brothers about one of those dreams, then everything seemed to fall apart.

His brothers threw him into a pit. Then they sold him to some merchants heading to Egypt, and the merchants sold him into slavery in that foreign land.

Ah, but then things began to look up again. His master was a great and wealthy man, and he so trusted Joseph that he turned over his entire estate to Joseph. What more could a guy expect?

But it wasn't to last. His master's wife falsely accused Joseph, and he ended up rotting in jail again. What else could go wrong? No doubt, he just couldn't understand what God was doing to him. He might have been tempted to throw up his hands and ask, "Why me, God?" Perhaps he was ready to throw in the towel.

That's life. Even as obedient Christians, sometimes things happen to us that we just can't understand. We lose our success, our family, our friends, our reputation, and even our confidence in God Himself. We're ready to give up on ourselves, life, and God.

Pictured above is the oldest house excavated in Bethany. It was almost certainly in existence when Jesus visited the city. You can see the low, narrow entrance that would have forced adults to stoop slightly in order to enter. Most houses were built of clay or mud brick. In some smaller homes two all-purpose rooms housed large extended families and sometimes even goats, sheep, and other animals at night.

Floors were bare earth, and ceilings were usually made of small branches laid across the walls with mud or clay mashed into the cracks and hardened by the sun. The roof was used for several purposes, including drying fruits and vegetables or as an evening respite from the uncomfortably hot first floor. A ladder or outside stairs provided access to the roof.

But that's because we're trying to understand God in terms of our human thinking. The Bible clearly tells us that God's ways are not our ways; we simply can't fathom how God works (Is. 55:8). It just as clearly tells us, however, that God works all things for our ultimate good and His glory (Rom. 8:28). If we trust His Word in Romans 8:28, we must accept the limitations of our own finite understanding and leave every aspect of our lives in His care, trusting Him to keep His Word and work everything out to His glory. And this confidence should, in turn, equip and encourage us to do exactly what God's called us to do for each moment—even when He seems to change His mind!

In this lesson, we will see that Christ did some things that the people, including His own disciples, simply didn't understand. But Christ was using those events to prepare the disciples for what they would face later at and after His crucifixion.

(For a more detailed examination of Joseph's response to the problems of life, read Robert E. Reccord's book *When Life Is the Pits*. Another book that is helpful in developing a proper response to problems in our pathway is *When God Interrupts* by M. Craig Barnes.)

Once again, as we begin this lesson, we find that John left a gap of between one and two months in the historical record. This time the gap occurs between the end of John 10 and the beginning of John 11. But Luke comes to our rescue and provides a record of the events that occurred during this gap. All of the events happened while Christ was in Perea during January A. D. 30. Read each of the following references and then record in the space beside each the event(s) that are recorded in that passage of Scripture.

Scripture reference	What happened
Luke 13:22–30	
Luke 13:31–35	
Luke 14:1–24	
Luke 14:25–35	
Luke 15:1–32	
Luke 16:1–17:10	Jesus taught three parables on stewardship, each directed to a specific audience: 1. To the disciples—the parable of the unjust steward 2. To the Pharisees—the parable of the rich man and Lazarus 3. To the disciples—the parable of the servant who made a meal for the master first before he himself ate

As we pick up the story in John again, we find that Christ was still in Perea.

Student Work

Read John 10:40–11:46.

Why do you think Jesus waited two days and allowed Lazarus to die?_____
_____
_____

How would this make you feel if you were Mary or Martha—or Lazarus? _____
_____
_____

Would you have changed your mind after you saw how things turned out? Why?_____
_____
_____
_____
_____

What do you think Martha meant when she said that she knew God would give Jesus whatever He asked? _____
_____
_____
_____

If you were an observer, what would have been your thoughts about Jesus as you saw Mary and Martha's grief? Would you have been angry with Jesus? _____
_____
_____

What would you have thought after Lazarus was resurrected?
_____
_____
_____

What did Jesus say was the purpose for Lazarus' resurrection?
_____
_____

This is not Lazarus' tomb, but it is a reconstruction of the exterior of a typical tomb from the first century A.D.

Do you think this was the most amazing sign of Jesus' deity to this point? If so, why? If not, what sign in the Gospel of John was more convincing to you? _____

_____

_____

_____

_____

Notes From The Teacher's Lesson

Christ Ministers In Perea And Bethany

In Perea (10:40–42)

- The _____ of John's ministry
- The _____ for us
  - We must sow and cultivate the seed; God gives the increase.
  - We may never see the results of our labor.

In Bethany (11:1–46)

- The _____ of God (vs. 1–6)
  - Not always our ways
  - Always perfectly best for us
- The _____ of the disciples (vs. 7–16)
  - Lack of courage (vs. 8)
  - Lack of understanding (vs. 12)
  - Lack of faith (vs. 16)
- The _____ of Martha (vs. 17–28)
  - Believes Christ will raise Lazarus
  - Does not comprehend *when*
- The _____ of Mary (vs. 28–32)
  - Does not consider Jesus' power to raise Lazarus
  - An "if only" Christian

- The _____ of Jesus (vs. 33–38)

  - His tears

  - His anger

- The _____ of Jesus (vs. 39–44)

  - Words move Lazarus

  - Word saves souls

- The _____ of the people (vs. 45–46)

  - Some to believe

  - Some not to believe

Digging Deeper

1. Read a biography of Hudson Taylor, William Carey, David Livingstone, Mary Slessor, or another missionary who labored long and hard to spread God's Word among the heathen before seeing any results from his or her labors. Illustrate from their lives' experience how one person might plant the seed, another water it or cultivate the soil, and still another person will reap the fruit in a soul's coming to salvation.

2. Explain the following statement: "Control what you can control—and let go of what you can't." Is that a true statement? Write a paper explaining what that statement means (or how it should be expressed) and how it should apply to the life of every believer.

3. Conduct a detailed study of one (or more) of the parables that Jesus taught in the time period covered by this lesson and/or the gap between John 10 and John 11. List the direct applications you can make to your own life from lessons taught in the parable(s).

4. Read John 11:18. A furlong is 606 feet, 9 inches. Based on that fact, calculate the distance from Bethany to Jerusalem. (Give your answer in furlongs, feet, and miles.) Use the map on page 278 to describe what that journey might have been like.

25
The Triumphal Entry

A girl sits in a field surrounded by bright white and yellow daisies. In fact, she's holding one daisy that she has picked from the field. As she holds its stem with one hand, she slowly plucks off the white petals with the fingers of her other hand.

"He loves me," she says as she plucks off one petal. "He loves me not." She plucks off another petal. "He loves me. He loves me not." On and on she goes until she comes to the last petal. "He loves me *not!*"

Her face takes on an expression of disgust, and she tosses the decimated flower over her shoulder. "Oh, he's so fickle!" she blurts out.

Fickle.

One dictionary defines "fickle" as "marked by lack of steadfastness, constancy, or stability; given to erratic and even perverse changeableness."

It isn't a very flattering term to have applied to you. In fact, it's a very bad trait to have, especially when it comes to spiritual things. Our friends, classmates, employers, and family members expect us to be dependable. When we behave inconsistently, however, we might be labeled "fickle." We're hard working one day and lazy the next. We're on time one day and late the next. We're fulfilling our responsibilities like eager beavers one day and then ambivalent about them the next.

Fickleness is especially bad when it affects our love and service for the Lord. We claim to love the Lord wholeheartedly, but how often our actions show that we don't really love Him enough to do what He expects of us. We

seem to be "sold out" and surrendered to His service sometimes, but then we rebel and try to retake control of our lives. When we're fickle about our relationship with Christ, we aren't really committed to Him at all.

That's the way the people of Jerusalem were during the last few days of Jesus' life. In this lesson, you will study how Jesus made a triumphal entry into Jerusalem. We call it the "triumphal entry" because of the way the people reacted to Him. They shouted, "Hosanna!" They strewed palm leaves in His path. They hailed Him as their king! He was the most popular man in Jerusalem that day.

But the people were fickle. The triumphal entry was on Sunday. By the following Thursday, those same people were yelling, "Crucify Him! Give us Barabbas!" They were ridiculing Him, mocking Him, and calling for His death.

What made the difference? They never really loved Him to begin with. Rather, they loved what they could get from Him: freedom from the Romans, free food, and miraculous healings. When they realized that He had not come to provide those things for them and that the tide of popular opinion was going against Him, they deserted Him.

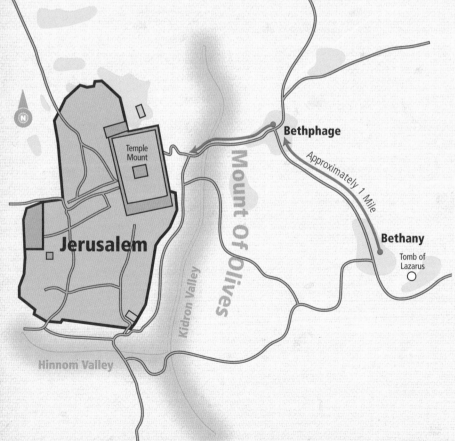

How about you? Do you *really* love the Lord enough to give yourself as a "living sacrifice" for Him? Or are you fickle, too? Ask yourself these questions as you study this lesson. Make certain your love for the Lord.

Once again, we must fill in a gap in John's account. This time, the gap occurs between John 11:46–47, and both Mark and Luke provide the record of the missing events. Read each of the following references and then write in the space beside each the event(s) recorded in that passage of Scripture. Note *where* each of the events occurred.

Scripture reference	What happened
Luke 17:11–37 (in Samaria or Galilee)	Christ healed ten lepers, but only one returned to thank/glorify Him
Luke 18:1–14	Christ taught two parables on prayer: 1. The widow who persisted in asking a judge to avenge her of her enemies 2. The publican and the Pharisee who prayed in the temple
Mark 10:1–12 (from Galilee to Perea)	Christ taught on…
Mark 10:13–16 (possibly in Perea)	
Mark 10:17–31 (in Perea)	
Mark 10:32–45 (in Perea)	
Mark 10:46–52 (at Jericho)	
Luke 19:1–28 (at Jericho)	

Student Work

Christ's choice of a donkey for his entrance to Jerusalem seems surprising to the modern mind. Today, donkeys are objects of derision, and horses are seen as the majestic animal. In Jesus' time horses were seldom used for personal transportation, reserved instead for use in war. Since kings were forbidden from collecting large numbers of horses (Deut 17:16), donkeys were often used by royalty. Mules (the cross between a horse and a donkey) were sometimes reserved exclusively for kings' use. Jesus' choice of a donkey was actually a bold statement of his kingship and deity.

Read John 11:45–12:1, 9–19.

The end of chapter 11 suggests that the Pharisees were motivated by their fear that the Romans would hear of Jesus' popularity and crack down on the nation. What does their emphasis on politics over truth communicate about their priorities? _____
_____
_____
_____

When Caiaphas spoke about one man's dying for the people, what did he intend to say would be the advantage of eliminating Jesus?
_____
_____
_____

Apparently Caiaphas prophesied without realizing it. What did his prophesy say about what would be the implications of Jesus' death? _____
_____
_____

If you were part of the multitude at the triumphal entry, what might you have thought was about to happen? _____
_____
_____
_____

How surprised would you have been with Jesus' crucifixion a week later? _____
_____

What would you have thought about a king riding on a donkey?
_____
_____
_____

What would this have communicated to you about the character of this entering king? _____
_____
_____

The view of the Mount of Olives in the background as seen from Bethphage and Bethany. Jesus would have walked from here over the Mount of Olives to Jerusalem on the other side.

Notes From The Teacher's Lesson

The Triumphal Entry

Caiaphas' _____ *Plan (11:47–52)*

- Sadducees grow _____ (vs. 47–48).

  - Public _____ in Christ's favor

  - Possibility of another _____

- Caiaphas solves the problem (vs. 49–50).

  - Proposes _____ Jesus to save the nation.

  - Philosophy: "The end _____ the means."

- Caiaphas makes an unwitting prophecy (vs. 52–53).

Jesus' Last _____ *From Public View (11:53–57)*

The Public's _____ *Interest (12:1, 9–11)*

- Crowds want to see Jesus and Lazarus.

- Pharisees want to kill Lazarus.

The King's _____ Entry (12:12–17)

- Seven steps of His entry
  - Walked from Bethany to Bethphage
  - Sent two disciples after a donkey
  - Received the donkey
  - Rode down the Mount of Olives
  - Hailed as King
  - Overcome with emotion and wept
  - Viewed the temple and then left
- The object ridden
  - Symbol of _____ and dependence on the Lord
  - Symbol of _____
  - Fulfillment of _____

The World's _____ (12:18–19)

- Hail Him as king one day
- Crucify Him four days later

Digging Deeper

1. John 12:19 closes with Jesus' triumphal entry into Jerusalem on Sunday. The next verse (vs. 20) has Jesus in Jerusalem the next afternoon. According to the following references, what happened Sunday night and Monday morning?

   Sunday evening

   - Mark 11:11; Matthew 21:17— _____
     _____

   Monday morning

   - Mark 11:12–14— _____

   - Mark 11:15–18— _____

   - Luke 19:45–48— _____

Unit 6

Christ's Private Ministry To His Disciples

26

Christ's Meeting With The Greeks

The speaker walked proudly toward the podium to deliver his address to the students at the Christian school assembly. He was a famous and important man with an important message, and he wanted to impress the students with those facts. He was self-confident and self-assured. He wanted the students to see these qualities and be impressed with him. He wanted to have them talk of him in glowing terms after his fabulous speech. He wanted to leave the school more important and more famous than he had entered it. This was his opportunity to shine! In short, we might say that he was "full of himself."

As he reached the pulpit and began to position his notes before him, however, his eyes were drawn to a shiny brass plaque attached to the surface of the pulpit just above where his notes lay. He spoke a brief word of greeting to the students and their teachers and then glanced more closely at the inscription on the plaque. It read, "Sirs, we would see Jesus."

Suddenly, those words pierced the speaker's heart with deep conviction. He realized that he had been concerned about presenting himself to the students. He wanted to impress them with his own importance, knowledge, wisdom, accomplishments, and fame. But the inscription on that plaque stopped him cold. These five words reminded him that people didn't want to see him; they wanted to see Jesus.

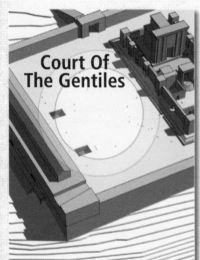

Court Of The Gentiles

At that moment, the speaker suddenly changed his message. Rather than sharing with the students how he had achieved such fame and importance and how wise and great *he* was, he confessed his pride to them and spoke to them about what Christ had done for him. His willingness to humble himself under the conviction of those simple but profound words allowed him to reach more students with Christ's message than all of the proud speakers' tricks he had originally planned to use to "wow" his audience.

How about you? When people see you, who do they *really* see? Do they see you and your accomplishments, looks, and personality? Or do they see Jesus shining through you? Whenever you find yourself getting "full of yourself," remember what the Greeks said to the disciples: "Sirs, we would see Jesus."

The events of John 12 are not in chronological order. For example, the events of John 12:9–50 occurred on Monday afternoon whereas the episode recorded in John 12:2–8 didn't happen until Tuesday evening (the Jewish Wednesday). What happened during the day on Tuesday, Nisan 12, A.D. 30? Discover the answer to the question by examining the following passages.

Early Morning:

Mark 11:19–25—The disciples saw a fig tree dried up and knew that it was the one that Christ cursed; He told them that they could have faith that would move mountains and that they should have a forgiving spirit.

Mid-Morning to Noon:

The Sanhedrin formally challenged Christ with the following four questions:

1. Matthew 21:23—By what power do you do these things? And who gave you that authority?

   Answer: Matthew 21:24–22:14—Was John's baptism from heaven or of men? They could not answer Him. Christ continued by teaching three parables.

2. Luke 20:20–22—Is it lawful for us to pay tribute to Caesar or not?

   Answer: Luke 20:23–26—Why do you test me? Show me a coin. Whose image and inscription is on it? Render to Caesar the things that are Caesar's and to God the things that are God's.

Matthew and Mark record the incident in which Jesus cursed a fruitless fig tree. This particular event occurred about the time of Passover, which was at least two months prior to the earliest fig harvest. Typical varieties of Palestinian figs produced two harvests each year, one in June and the second in August. Jesus cursed the tree to illustrate Israel's un-fruitfulness and future judgment, not because of particular animosity towards that tree.

3. Luke 20:27–33—If a brother dies with no children and another brother marries his wife, whose wife will she be in the resurrection?

   Answer: Luke 20:34–40—There is no marrying or dying in heaven. God is the God of the living.

4. Mark 12:28—Which is the first commandment of all?

   Answer: Mark 12:29–34—The Lord our God is one Lord. You must love the Lord your God with all your heart, soul, mind, and strength.

Noon:

Mark 12:35–37—Jesus now silenced the Pharisees with the following questions: How say the scribes that Christ is the Son of David? David called Him Lord, how is Christ then his son?

Afternoon:

- Matthew 23:1–39—His last public speech, given to the multitude and His disciples to observe the bidding of the Pharisees but not to participate in sin; don't do things just to be seen of men or out of pride.

- Mark 13:1–2—Leaving the temple, He taught the disciples about the great building. No stone will be left on top of another, but it will all be thrown down.

- Matthew 24:3–25:46—Arriving at the Mount of Olives, He taught as follows: Olivet discourse; Daniel's seventieth week; the abomination of desolation; the King's return to earth following the Tribulation.

- Matthew 26:1–5—Heading for Bethany on Tuesday evening, He told the disciples that in two days He would be betrayed to be crucified; chief priest and scribes and elders will gather to decide how to take Jesus and kill Him.

John resumes the story with the Tuesday evening (the Jewish Wednesday) meal at the home of Simon in John 12:2.

Student Work

Read John 12:20–50.

Why do you think some Greeks would have been coming to worship at the feast and searching for Jesus? _____

_____

_____

_____

How do Jesus' statements about glorification in verse 23 and death in verse 24 fit together? _____

_____

_____

_____

How does Jesus apply this principle to believers? _____

_____

_____

What attitude about yourself must you have before your life can be fruitful? _____

_____

Jesus said His soul was troubled. What do you think affected Him *most* of all that He was about to face? _____

_____

_____

_____

What would you have done if you were one of the believing rulers who feared the Pharisees and wanted their approval? Would you have hesitated to confess Christ publicly? _____

_____

_____

_____

_____

Do you think these rulers were believers? Why or why not?

_____

_____

_____

_____

What do the last few verses of this passage suggest about Jesus' personal ambition? What motivated him to do and say what he did? _____

_____

_____

_____

 ## Notes from the Teacher's Lesson

Christ's Meeting with the Greeks

The Events Of Monday, Nisan 11

- Condemns the fig tree (Matt. 21:19–22; Mark 11:12–14)

- Casts out moneychangers from the temple (Matt. 21:12–17; Mark 11:15–19; Luke 19:45–48)

- Heals the blind and the lame (Luke 19:47–48)

The Greeks Seek Jesus (12:20–22).

- Most likely proselytes—_____ converts to Judaism

- First Gentiles interested in Christ

Jesus' Answer (12:23–50)

- Jesus' words to the _____ (vs. 23–26)

  - Arrival of "His hour"

  - Looks toward the Church

- Jesus' words to the _____ (vs. 27–28)

- Jesus' words to the _____ (vs. 31–36, 44–50)

  - The purposes of His death (vs. 31–33)

    - Final triumph over Satan

    - Draw all men to Himself

  - The purposes of His life (vs. 34–36; 44–50)

    - To give light

- To save the world

- To obey the Father

- The people's _____ to Jesus' words (vs. 37–43)

  - Unbelief (vs. 37–41)

  - Belief without _____ (vs. 42–43)

Digging Deeper

1. Conduct a study of Psalm 22, comparing its contents with the description of Christ's death on the Cross in the various Gospels. Read what Charles Spurgeon wrote about this psalm in *The Treasury of David* (vol. 1, pp. 324 ff.).

2. The people said to Jesus' disciples, "Sirs, we would see Jesus." Do people see Jesus in your life? Would they know—from watching your life from day to day—that you could point them to the Savior? List steps that you can take to ensure that people recognize you as being a true disciple of Jesus Christ. What does 1 Peter 3:15 say about this Christian obligation? How can you equip yourself to live that verse?

3. Explain (using Scripture) what Christ meant when He said, "As Moses lifted up the serpent in the wilderness…" (John 12:24).

4. Compare Christ's words "My soul is troubled" (John 12:27) with His experience in the Garden of Gethsemane.

5. Christ spoke of His soul only three times in Scripture, one of which is in John 12:27. Locate and describe the settings of the other two instances. What do all three instances have in common?

27

Christ's Conflicts With The Pharisees

Marissa had a beautiful soprano voice. She had participated in numerous choirs and ensembles during high school. She had taken voice lessons from an accomplished teacher and was trained in music. In fact, she had won a number of musical competitions and had even been asked to play the leading role in a community production of a popular musical. Even music critics were saying that she was a shoo-in for a fantastic musical career in opera.

Richard was a born leader. Popular and vivacious, outgoing and sociable, he was liked by everyone in the school and community. He was elected to major class offices every year and was the president of both the student body and his church youth group during his senior year. He was a gifted organizer and was a pro at accounting. In fact, several civic groups offered him full scholarships if he would pursue a career in business administration at the local state college.

Everyone was shocked when Marissa turned down a sure future in opera. They were even more shocked when Richard politely refused the scholarships.

Were these gifted young people crazy? Why were they ruining their lives?

But neither Marissa nor Richard looked upon their decisions as ruining their lives. Rather, they were simply following the leading of the Lord, and He didn't want them to pursue opera or business. Instead, they were

willing to sacrifice those promising careers because what they wanted more was to serve God first with their lives.

Marissa became a Christian school music teacher, and she's now training other young ladies to sing with quality voices for the glory of God. She also sings in her church's choir and often provides solos that help prepare the listeners' hearts to hear the preaching of the Word of God. She's not famous as far as the world is concerned, but she's doing what God called her to do and using her gifts for God's glory.

Richard attended a Christian college and studied for the ministry. He is now an effective preacher and the administrator of a small Christian school. In those positions, he finds ample opportunities to use his organizational and financial skills. On the side, he also conducts financial seminars in which he helps young couples develop and apply principles of wise financial stewardship. He's not making as much money as he could make in the business world, but he's laying up treasures in heaven.

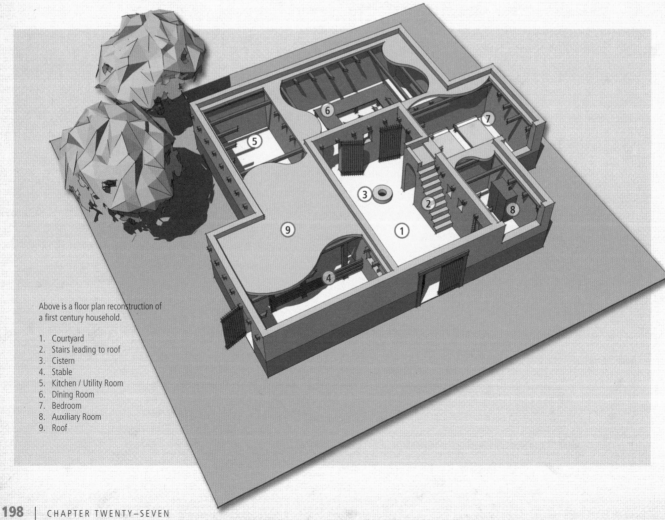

Above is a floor plan reconstruction of a first century household.

1. Courtyard
2. Stairs leading to roof
3. Cistern
4. Stable
5. Kitchen / Utility Room
6. Dining Room
7. Bedroom
8. Auxiliary Room
9. Roof

"What a waste!" some people might say of these two young people. But they are not wasting anything. In fact, they're investing wisely in things that *really* matter. They are touching lives rather than amassing fame and fortune for themselves.

In this lesson you'll see how Mary used what she had to honor Christ sacrificially. How could you best glorify God by using the gifts He's given you?

Read the following passages and fill in the gaps in John's record of events.

Tuesday night:

- Luke 22:3–6—After the evening meal, Judas, stung by Jesus' rebuke, left to confer with the chief priests and captains on how he might betray Christ in the absence of the multitude. He is offered money.

Wednesday morning:

- Mark 14:12–16— Christ sent two disciples into the city to inquire after the owner of a house where they can prepare for the Passover feast.

Wednesday evening:

- Mark 14:17; Luke 22:14–16; 24:30—Jesus sat down with His disciples to eat the Passover meal.

Student Work

Matthew 21:23–27

 Why would Jesus answer the religious leaders' question with another question rather than simply answering it directly? _____
_____
_____

 What do the leaders' private discussion and final answer show about the strength of their convictions? _____
_____
_____

Both Roman and Jewish coins were in circulation in Judea during the first half of the first century A.D. Although the vast majority would have been the local Jewish coins, the Roman tax needed to be paid in Roman currency.

Julius Caesar was the first living Roman Emperor to mint a coin with his image molded in it. Tiberius was emperor during Jesus' adult life. Since he also minted a coin with his image, his silver denarius is probably the coin Jesus referred to as "that which is Caesar's." Its value was about one day's wage. An inscription on this coin paying tribute to Tiberius' father Augustus Caesar would have been particularly repulsive to the Jews, since Augustus had been proclaimed to be deity.

Luke 20:19–26

How was the religious leaders' private plotting different from their public conversation with Jesus? _____

What do you think Luke means when he says they marveled at (or were amazed by) his answer? _____

Mark 12:28–34

Why do you think everyone was too intimidated to ask more questions of Jesus after this incident? _____

Did Jesus do something to scare them, or did they have another reason? _____

John 12:2–8

If you were an observer when Mary anointed Jesus' feet, would you have sided with Judas or Mary? (Imagine you don't know about what John says in verse 6.) _____

What do you think motivated Mary to sacrifice an item worth a year's wages? _____

How is your life characterized by that motivation? _____

Notes From The Teacher's Lesson

Christ's Conflicts With The Pharisees

The Events Of Tuesday, Nisan 12: Four Test Questions

- Christ's _____ (Matt. 21:23–27)

- Christ and _____ (Luke 20:19–26)

- Christ and the _____ (Luke 20:27–38)

- Christ and the _____ (Mark 12:28–34)

Jesus Takes The Initiative.

- Reveals their _____

- Rebukes their _____

Jesus Teaches On The Mount Of Olives.

Jesus Arrives In Bethany.

Jesus Eats The Supper At Bethany.

- The _____ of one who truly loves the Lord

- The _____ of one who pretends to love the Lord

- The _____ of Jesus: He knows men's hearts.

Digging Deeper

1. The Pharisees questioned Jesus' authority to do what He did. Similarly, down through history, the leaders of the world's political and religious hierarchies have questioned the authority of Christian ministers, missionaries, and educators. Cite examples of famous Christians who continued to minister faithfully in spite of such challenges concerning their authority, licensure, ecclesiastical approval, etc.

2. Write a paper explaining the proper Christian response to taxation by the government. Use as your primary biblical support Christ's teaching in Luke 20:19–26, but offer other Scripture proofs as applicable.

3. Conduct a study of the Sadducees. Focus especially on their rejection of the idea of a resurrection. If they did not believe in the resurrection, why did they ask Jesus whose wife the woman who had outlasted seven husbands would be?

4. What does the apostle Paul say of our hope if there is no resurrection? Why is the doctrine of the resurrection of Christ central to Christianity? What did Job say that revealed his belief in the resurrection?

5. List practical lessons to be learned from the self-sacrificial gift of Mary in lavishing a bottle of costly perfume on the Lord.

28

Christ's Last Supper

The little boy sat mesmerized as he watched the strange things that were happening around him. The members of the small church to which his parents belonged were celebrating the Lord's Supper, or communion, as some people called it. The men and boys of the church sat at a long table on one side of the small church's basement. The women and girls of the church sat at a similar table on the opposite side of the basement.

In front of each adult at both tables was a plate. Serving plates held stacks of light bread. Serving bowls contained a gravy-like liquid that they called "the sop." After a prayer of thanksgiving, the adults dipped the slices of bread into the sop, placed them on their plates, and then ate them. The little boy recalled thinking how gross that gravy must have tasted!

After everyone had eaten their sop-soaked bread, the preacher directed them to the next part of the service. Every other adult bent down and began to wash the feet of the person sitting next to him or her and then dried them with a towel. This ceremony continued until every church member's feet had been washed by someone.

Next, the preacher distributed portions of long strips of unleavened bread to the adults and older children. The little boy recognized these bread strips because he had seen his mother baking them earlier that day. Then the preacher spoke for a few moments and read some verses of Scripture. Then everyone ate the strips of bread. Finally, they each drank some grape juice from some little tiny glasses.

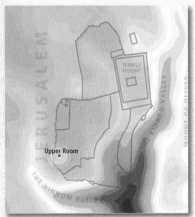

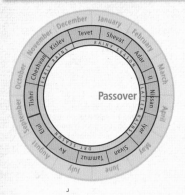

The little boy didn't understand much of what was going on, but he knew that it was a time during which the adults were very serious and thoughtful. It was definitely not a time for a little boy to misbehave in church! As tedious as the ceremony was for him, he enjoyed eating the leftover bread strips after the service. They didn't have much taste, but it was the only part of the ceremony that he really understood—he finally got to eat!

Not all churches practice the ceremony that that little boy witnessed, but they generally practice some aspects of celebrating communion, or the Lord's Supper. As even that little boy knew, it is a solemn and serious commemoration of the death of Jesus Christ for us. How serious it is was the subject of some of Paul's writings, especially 1 Corinthians 11. Paul warned in that passage, "Wherefore whosoever shall eat this bread, and drink this cup of the Lord, unworthily, shall be guilty of the body and blood of the Lord. But let a man examine himself, and so let him eat of that bread, and drink of that cup. For he that eateth and drinketh unworthily, eateth and drinketh damnation to himself, not discerning the Lord's body" (vs. 27–29).

Communion is an important part of the life of a Christian. It is a corporate reminder to the church that is to be done "in remembrance of Me." When you participate in the Lord's Supper, do you do so seriously and introspectively? Do you come to the Lord's Table only after first seeking forgiveness from both the Lord and other believers whom you have offended in some way or who have offended you? Are you taking full advantage to re-center your life and heart on Christ and the incomparable work He has accomplished?

Before you partake of communion the next time, think seriously of what you're doing. Examine yourself carefully, confess any sin that might cause you to eat and drink unworthily, and then remember what the ceremony symbolizes.

Student Work

Read John 13:1–38.

 Why do you think Peter resisted Jesus washing his feet?

_____

_____

_____

✎ What attitude did he show in his resistance? _____
_____

✎ What attitude did it take for Peter to yield and allow his teacher and master to continue? _____
_____

✎ Why do you think Jesus would have permitted an unbeliever to infiltrate His inner circle of disciples? _____
_____
_____

✎ The events seem to show plainly that Judas was the betrayer. If you were one of the disciples, what might have made you think that he was leaving to take care of the group's business? _____
_____
_____

✎ If you were Peter, how would you have felt when you heard Jesus predict that you would deny Him? _____
_____
_____

Notes From The Teacher's Lesson

Christ's Last Supper

The Occasion (13:1)

- The _____ Passover

- The _____ Passover

  - Afternoon of Nisan 14: lamb slain

  - Evening of Nisan 15: lamb roasted and ceremony begins

The Passover Lamb (13:1–30)

- Christ's _____ (vs. 1–3)

  - Knows His hour is come (vs. 1)

  - Knows His betrayer and what he is about to do (vs. 2)

  - Knows His own identity (vs. 3)

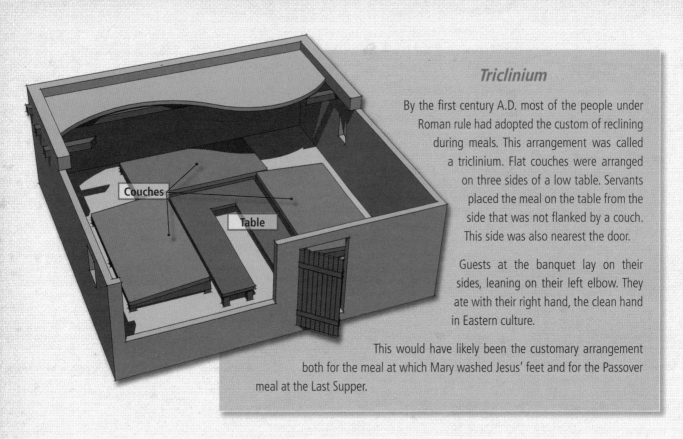

Triclinium

By the first century A.D. most of the people under Roman rule had adopted the custom of reclining during meals. This arrangement was called a triclinium. Flat couches were arranged on three sides of a low table. Servants placed the meal on the table from the side that was not flanked by a couch. This side was also nearest the door.

Guests at the banquet lay on their sides, leaning on their left elbow. They ate with their right hand, the clean hand in Eastern culture.

This would have likely been the customary arrangement both for the meal at which Mary washed Jesus' feet and for the Passover meal at the Last Supper.

Couches

Table

- Christ's _____ (vs. 4–12)

- Christ's _____ (vs. 21, 23–30)

  - Broken and compassionate toward Judas

  - Honors Judas by offering him the sop

The Disciples (13:31–38)

- Peter's rash statements

  - _____ wash my feet (vs. 8)

  - Not _____ my feet (vs. 9)

  - Lay down my _____ (vs. 37)

- The disciples' _____ (vs. 22)

- The disciples' _____ (vs. 31–38)

- The disciples' complete _____ (vs. 38)

Digging Deeper

1. Explain and illustrate the following statement: "Behind every wrongful act is a need in someone's life."

2. Note the times when Peter swung from one extreme to another. What practical steps will help you avoid being like that?

3. Conduct an in-depth study of the life of Peter using as your guide Kenneth Frederick's book *The Making of a Disciple: A Study of Discipleship* from the Life of Simon Peter.

4. Study denominations that practice foot washing. Why do they do so? What Scripture support do they offer for the practice? What historical precedent (other than the example of Christ) do they offer for the practice? Do you agree or disagree with the practice. Why?

5. Read and report on the specified chapter in one of the following books: "The Passover Lamb" in Robert T. Ketcham's *Old Testament Pictures of New Testament Truth*, or "Passover and the Lord's Supper" in Victor Buksbazen's *The Gospel in the Feasts of Israel*.

29
Christ's Last Words
And Promises

"What's in a name?" William Shakespeare asked in his play *Romeo and Juliet.*

Apparently, there's a lot in a name. Just notice the lengths to which people will go to protect a good name or to cover a bad name. Many Hollywood actors and actresses even change their names from something that they consider boring to names that are more exciting and memorable.

Companies believe that their names are so important that they go to the trouble and expense of registering them as trademarks, and they fight hard to preserve the recognition of those trademarks. Any company that is lax in protecting its name or trademark risks having it become a generic term that anyone can use or apply to any number of uses. For example, paper products manufacturer Kimberly-Clark fights hard to prevent its brand name Kleenex® from being used as a generic term for facial tissues. They frequently sue people who have violated that registered trademark—all to protect their corporate name.

The need for protecting a name is also important for anyone who claims the name *Christian*. There are certain characteristics that people just expect to be evident in the life of such a person, and if one is careless with that name and how he lives his life, he risks dishonoring the name *Christian*.

For example, one popular fad is for people to wear or display various items—from bracelets to T-shirts to bumper stickers—sporting the initials

WWJD: *What Would Jesus Do?* The wearers or bearers of that slogan, however, must realize that their behavior can actually negate its message if the behavior doesn't match what Jesus would really do. It's true that "actions speak louder than words"—or bracelets.

Have you ever been driving and had a car bearing a WWJD bumper sticker rudely and dangerously cut you off on the highway? Have you ever heard a person wearing a WWJD bracelet or T-shirt curse or use the Lord's name in vain? It happens far too often, and unbelievers notice it, believe me!

What's the magic of a name? There is no magic. But a name can be very powerful—either for good or for bad. Remember who you are as a believer, and act, talk, and think in such a way as to bring honor to your "family name"—Christian. Protect that trademark!

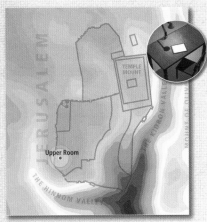

Student Work

Read John 14:1–31.

Imagine that you were one of Jesus' disciples who had just heard Jesus predict that Peter would deny him. How would you have felt when the next words He spoke were encouragement to be at peace and trust in Him?_____
_____
_____
_____

Where do you suppose Thomas thought Jesus was going?_____
_____
_____

Describe the promised ministry of the Holy Spirit to the disciples in your own words._____
_____
_____
_____
_____
_____

What is the difference between Jesus' promise of peace and the world's offer of peace?_____
_____
_____
_____

After all the different times John has said the disciples believed in Jesus, he says in verse 29 that they would believe when they saw His prophecies come true. What does Jesus mean by this new use of the word "believe"? _____

_____

_____

_____

How was Jesus going to show the world that He loved the Father?

_____

_____

Notes From The Teacher's Lesson

Christ's Last Words And Promises

A Future _____ Place (14:1–11)

- Where heaven is
- How to get to heaven
  - Christ is the _____ .
  - Christ is the _____ .
  - Christ is the _____ .
- _____ of heaven (vs. 7–11)

Power Through _____ (14:12–14)

- The power of the gospel
- The power of prayer
  - Necessity (Jas. 4:2)
  - In Christ's name
  - Glorifying the Father (vs. 13)

The Holy Spirit (14:15–18)

- Jesus, the _____
- Another _____
  - Jesus is about to leave them.
  - Jesus will send the Holy Spirit to them.
- The _____

Peace (14:27)

- The world's _____
  - The "peace" of temporary _____
  - The "peace" of _____
  - The "peace" of false _____
- Christ's peace
  - Permanent
  - Based on faith

 ## Digging Deeper

1. Explain what it means to pray "in Jesus' name."

2. Explain the seeming contradiction in the statements that our prayers must be according to the will of God, yet God will give us the desires of our heart. How are those two goals reconciled?

3. Conduct a study of the word vanity ("emptiness") in Ecclesiastes. Explain the lessons that Solomon is communicating through that book.

4. Read and write a summary report on one of the following classic works on prayer: *Power through Prayer* by E. M. Bounds, *How to Pray* by R. A. Torrey, or *With Christ in the School of Prayer* by Andrew Murray.

5. In John 14:16 Jesus called the Holy Spirit "another of the same kind of Comforter" (lit.). How is the Holy Spirit like Jesus in His ministry to and through the Christian? List as many similarities as you can.

30

Christ's Lesson On The Vine And The Branches

Nothing tasted better to Dale on a cold winter morning than his mother's hot, homemade biscuits topped with a large portion of her homemade Concord grape jelly, jam, or preserves. Just thinking of it made his mouth water.

But that tasty treat didn't just happen. A lot of work went into making it possible. His mother, of course, had to can the jam and the jelly, working for hours in a very hot kitchen (during the heat of summer—and without the benefit of air conditioning!). Before that, she had to pick the clusters of purple grapes from the vines, braving all sorts of bees, yellow jackets, and other pesky biting insects who were also wanting their share of the sweet juice and pulp.

But long before any of those clusters of grapes even began growing on the vine, Dale's father had to do his part to make the grape jelly, jam, or preserves possible. Before the grapes began producing, he had to examine the vines closely to determine which branches were broken, weak, diseased, or damaged. Then he took pruning shears and began to cut away the bad branches. Dale's responsibility was to gather all of the discarded branches, pile them into a heap, and then burn them.

At first, Dale didn't understand why this task was necessary. Wouldn't they get even more grapes next year if they left all of those branches on the vine? Then his father explained to him that all those bad branches did was sap

the other good branches of their nourishment from the root and the larger part of the vine. By cutting away, or pruning, the branches, his father was allowing more of the life-giving, grape-producing nutrients to flow to the good branches. That, in turn, guaranteed a much larger harvest than if they left all of the branches—both good and bad—intact.

Jesus used a similar illustration in the lesson you are about to study now. He said that for His children to bear fruit effectively, God must "prune" them, cutting out what is bad or a drain on their spiritual vitality and thereby allowing His life-giving graces to flow unhindered into the believers' lives. As they respond to that pruning process, He enables them to "bear much fruit."

How is God pruning your life right now? Are you resisting His wise pruning? Or are you trusting in His wisdom to bring forth even greater fruit for His glory?

Student Work

Read John 15:1–27.

What does it mean to prune a branch? _____
_____

Why would a gardener do this to a fruitful branch? _____
_____
_____

What does this passage teach us about our ability to perform good works? _____
_____
_____
_____

What do you think Jesus means by His command to "abide" (or "remain") in Him? _____
_____
_____
_____

What kinds of people are those who do not abide in Him, do not bear fruit, and are cast into the fire? _____
_____

What is the purpose for Jesus' commands and warnings in this passage? _____ _____ _____

What is the fruit in the life of the believer that He wants to be overflowing? _____ _____ _____

What do you think was on Jesus' mind when he spoke the words of verse 13?_____ _____ _____

Grapes were a significant commodity in the Judean agricultural society. It is likely that His disciples would have been quite familiar with vineyards and the care of grapevines from their extensive travel in Palestine.

Husbandmen were responsible for maximizing the quality and quantity of the grape harvest in their vineyard. In John 15 Jesus taught his disciples about the fruit the Father was producing in their lives. His metaphor focuses on the union of the vine and the branches. Branches depended on the vine for support and nourishment. Branches were worthless if they were separated from the vine.

The husbandman removed dead branches so they would not sap nutrients from the fruitful branches. These dead branches were taken away and destroyed by fire. Fruitful branches were cut back, or pruned, so that they would not grow too much and divert nutrients into the vegetation rather than the fruit. The husbandman's objective was to create balance between vegetative growth and fruit production in order to increase the crop.

If you were a disciple, what would you have thought about those words when you remembered them a year later? _____

_____

_____

_____

What is the attitude of worldly people towards you? _____

_____

Do they know enough about your faith in Christ to hate you as they hate Jesus? _____

Notes From The Teacher's Lesson

Christs Lesson On The Vine And The Branches

The Disciples' Responsibility (15:1–17)

- Bear fruit (vs. 1–8)

    - Nature of the fruit

        - _____

        - _____

        - _____

    - Production of the fruit

        - By being _____ daily with the Word (vs. 2–3)

        - By _____ in Christ (vs. 4–7)

- Love the brethren (vs. 9–17)

The World's Persecution (15:18–25)

- Persecution: the companion of _____ (vs. 18)

- Christians: automatically rejected just as Christ was rejected (vs. 18–20)

- Christians: unlike the _____ (vs. 19)

The Holy Spirit's Coming (15:26–27)

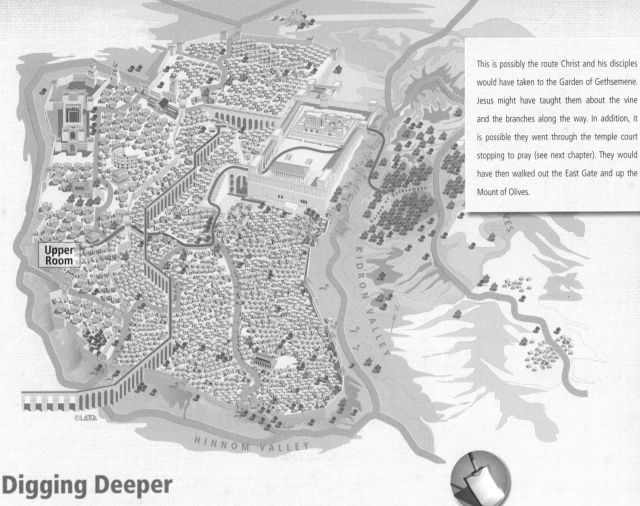

This is possibly the route Christ and his disciples would have taken to the Garden of Gethsemene. Jesus might have taught them about the vine and the branches along the way. In addition, it is possible they went through the temple court stopping to pray (see next chapter). They would have then walked out the East Gate and up the Mount of Olives.

Digging Deeper

1. Explain in practical terms what it means to "abide in Christ." Describe the obstacles to abiding in Christ. What steps can you take to overcome those obstacles?

2. Explain (using Scripture support) why the world has always persecuted Christians. What should be the Christian's reaction and response to persecution? What role does the Holy Spirit play in the life of the Christian who is suffering persecution?

3. Conduct a "fruit inspection" of your life. Are you producing fruit? If not, why not? If you are producing fruit, what steps can you take to ensure that you not only continue bearing fruit but also will increase that production? What are the keys to successful fruitbearing?

4. What lessons did Christ and John the Baptist teach concerning the importance of self sacrifice in the fruit-bearing process?

5. Who are the branches in John 15? What is suggested about the branches that are cut away and burned? What kind of a warning should this be to those who profess salvation?

31
Christ's Intercessory Prayer

A lot of people keep a prayer list in their Bibles so that they have ready access to it and can pray for special needs whenever they have the opportunity. The big advantage of using a prayer list, of course, is that it helps jog our memory. We have so many things about which to pray that it's often very difficult to remember them all, and when we forget to pray for something, we feel guilty.

So the prayer list is a tool to help us avoid the problem of forgetfulness. But what about the times when we don't have our Bible and the prayer list with us? We should always be in a position to pray, but how can we do that if we don't have that prayer list with us? How can our forgetful minds remember everything about which we should be praying?

You might not realize it, but you have a ready-made prayer list right on top of your neck! Even when you don't have your paper prayer list with you, you always have this handy prayer list with you! It's the features of your face!

Use each feature to remind you to pray for specific things. Consider carefully what we mean.

- Eyes—Of course, we see with our eyes. Your eyesight can help you to remember to pray for the people you see most—your parents, your brothers and/or sisters, and your close friends and relatives.

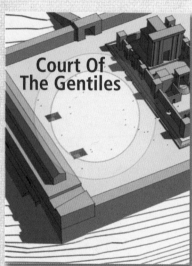

Court Of The Gentiles

- Mouth—Think of the times you've heard God speak to you through the preaching or teaching of His Word by your pastor, a missionary speaker, or your teachers. They used their mouths to communicate that message. When you see or use your mouth, it should help remind you to pray for the preachers, teachers, missionaries, and others in positions of spiritual leadership. Prompted by that general reminder, you should have little trouble thinking of specific peoples' names and needs.

- Ears—Hebrews 13:17 tells us to obey those who have authority over us. How can we obey them if we don't listen? Your ears should remind you of those who are over you in authority. That could include the rulers of our own national, state, and local government and your school principal. Paul instructs us to pray for those who are in authority over us so that we can live a quiet, peaceable life in godliness and spread the gospel to the world around us.

- Hair—Hair is a facial feature? Well, cut us a little slack on this one. Your hair is the most frail and transient feature of your head. It falls out all the time, and sometimes it doesn't grow back! If it does, it's probably going to turn gray sooner or later. The frailty of your hair should remind you to pray for the weak, the sick, the invalids, the spiritually immature, or oppressed people in your life or community.

- Nose—If something smells bad, your nose will tell you. If you stink spiritually, the noses of the people around you will tell them about it, too. Although we should be thinking in prayer of others more than ourselves, we must not be guilty of failing to pray for ourselves. One of the major emphases of our prayers should be that our lives might become a sweet smelling aroma to God.

Now you have no excuse for not praying—even if you forget or lose your paper prayer list! Why not give it a try? Use this prayer list memory tool to remind you of those for whom you should be praying.

After Christ's high priestly prayer, He was ready to enter the Garden of Gethsemane for His last moments with the disciples. Read the following passages and describe the event recorded in detail.

 Mark 14:26, 32–42; Luke 22:39–46— _____

_____

_____

_____

_____

_____

_____

_____

_____

_____

_____

_____

_____

Jesus was suddenly interrupted by the arrival of Judas Iscariot and the mob. John 18:2 picks up the story.

Student Work

Read John 17:1–26.

What do you think Jesus means when He says that eternal life is knowing the Father and Jesus Christ? _____

_____

_____

_____

What does Jesus' statement of how He glorified God suggest about how we can do likewise? _____

_____

_____

_____

What do you think Jesus meant when He said that the Father gave men (the disciples) to Jesus out of the world? _____

_____

_____

_____

What does verse 17 suggest the Word of God accomplishes in our lives? How does it make us different from what we have been? ___

_____

_____

_____

Imagine that you were one of the disciples hearing this prayer on your behalf. What part of the prayer would have had the greatest impact on you? Why?_____

_____

_____

_____

_____

 Christ prays for future believers in addition to the disciples. Since that includes us today, what part of this prayer do you think is most important for our time? _____

_____

_____

_____

Today Jews offer prayers at the western wall that remains from Herod's temple, also know as the Wailing Wall. This is one of the most emotional sites in present day Palestine because the sense of sorrow and loss at the state of God's chosen people is so plainly evident.

Notes From The Teacher's Lesson

Christ's Intercessory Prayer

Christ Prays For _____ *(17:1–8)*

- The finished work (vs. 4)
  - Christ had given eternal life to the disciples (vs. 2–3).
  - Christ had taught the disciples (vs. 6, 8).
  - The disciples had _____ the Word (vs. 8).
  - The disciples had _____ the Word (vs. 8).
- Two requests
  - To be glorified in His _____ (vs. 1)
  - To be glorified in the _____ of the Father (vs. 5)

Christ Prays For His _____ *(17:9–19).*

- Keep them (vs. 11–12)
- Sanctify them (vs. 17–19)

  - _____
  - _____
  - _____

Christic *Christ Prays For All Future* _____ *(17:20–26).*

- That we might be _____ (vs. 21–23)

  - With the Father and the Son (vs. 21)

  - With each other (vs. 22)

- That we might be one with Him in _____ (vs. 24)

Digging Deeper

1. Conduct a study of the prayers of Christ. Make a table or chart that describes those prayers. Focus particularly on Christ's prayers for (a) Himself, (b) His disciples, and (c) all future believers. What lessons do Christ's prayers teach us about our own prayers?

2. Conduct a study of the model prayer offered by Christ (generally called "The Lord's Prayer"). Explain the principles that Christ was teaching in each of the phrases contained in that prayer.

3. Do you have a prayer list of people or issues about which you pray regularly? If not, develop one. If you already have such a list, explain how it is helpful to your prayer life.

4. Read and report on one of the classic works on prayer that are included in the Recommended Reading List.

5. Read a biography of E. M. Bounds, who was famous for his life of prayer. Explain the effect that the practice of earnest and regular prayer had on his life and ministry.

6. Explain each aspect of the following statement by E. M. Bounds: "Behind the praying there must lie the conditions of prayer… Prayer does not stand alone. It is not an isolated performance. Prayer is connected to all the duties of the Christian life."

7. Read E. M. Bounds' book *Guide to Spiritual Warfare*, and explain the role that prayer plays on the spiritual battlefield.

Unit 7

Christ's Passion

32

Christ's Betrayal, Arrest, and Trial

Pontius Pilate was the fifth procurator (governmental representative) of Rome in Palestine. He held that office from A.D. 26–36. His name, Pontius, was his family name; the title Pilate meant "one armed with a javelin."

Little is known of Pilate's early life except for a few legends, which might or might not be true. He was said to be the illegitimate son of Tyrus. In Rome, he allegedly committed murder and was exiled to Asia Minor, where he subdued a rebellious people, thereby regaining the favor of Rome, and was awarded the governorship of Judea.

Pilate seemed to enjoy tormenting the Jews. He never seemed to understand them, and as the Jewish historian Josephus pointed out, he offended them by bringing idolatrous Roman standards into the city of Jerusalem. Another time, he hung gold shields inscribed with the names of the Roman gods on the temple itself. He also had his soldiers kill some Galileans while they were sacrificing in the temple. Luke 13:1 refers to that very incident: "There were present at that season some that told him of the Galileans, whose blood Pilate had mingled with their sacrifices."

Pilate's actual headquarters was in Caesarea, but he came to Jerusalem every Passover to keep order among the population, which swelled at that holiday. After the Jewish leaders condemned Christ, they brought Him to Pilate, who was probably living in Herod's palace near the temple, early in the morning.

From the beginning of the hearing, he was torn between offending the Jews again and condemning an innocent person. He tried every way of which he could think to convince the Jews to release Jesus. He didn't want them to complain to Rome again about his behavior so, putting politics before justice, he finally gave in to their demand to crucify Him.

According to Josephus, Pilate's political career ended six years later when he tried to suppress a small rebellion in Samaria and killed an innocent man. The Samaritans complained, and Pilate was recalled to Rome. His name then seems to have disappeared from official Roman governmental history. The historian Eusebius says, however, that soon afterward, "wearied with misfortune," he took his own life. One tradition says that he committed suicide in Vienna, whereas another legend says that he was banished to a mountain (now known as Mount Pilatus) on Lake Lucern in Switzerland. There, he allegedly plunged into the lake and to his death from a precipice. (The preceding information was taken from *Zondervan's Pictorial Bible Dictionary.*)

This Pilate was the man before whom Jesus stood condemned. As you study this lesson, consider how Jesus must have felt standing before such a notorious man.

Student Work

Read John 18.

What emotions do you think Judas may have been feeling as he stood with the crowd that was arresting Jesus? _____
_____
_____
_____

If you were one of the soldiers, what would have amazed you most about the scene in the garden? _____
_____
_____
_____

What might have caused Peter to deny that he knew Jesus? _____
_____
_____
_____

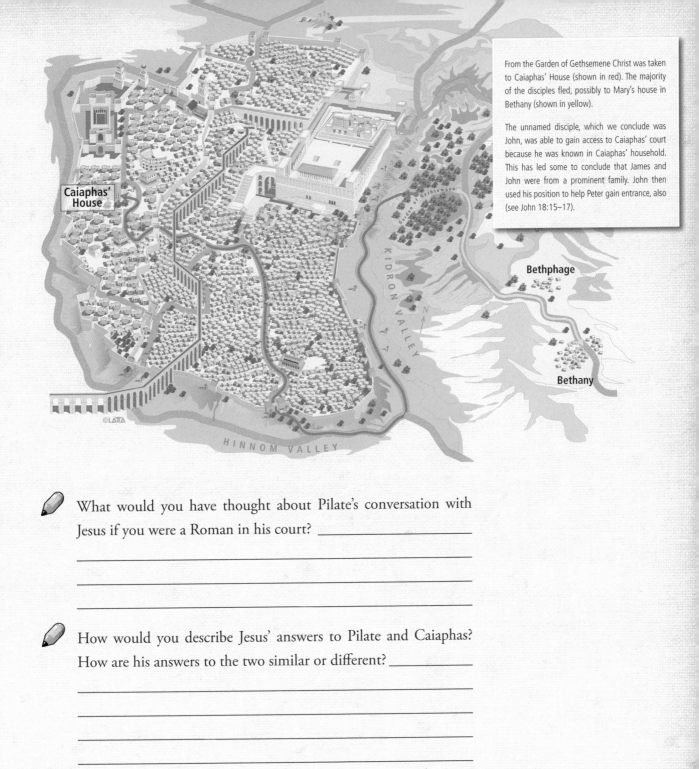

Caiaphas'
House

Bethphage

Bethany

KIDRON VALLEY

Garden of Gethsemene

N

HINNOM VALLEY

©LAITA

From the Garden of Gethsemene Christ was taken to Caiaphas' House (shown in red). The majority of the disciples fled, possibly to Mary's house in Bethany (shown in yellow).

The unnamed disciple, which we conclude was John, was able to gain access to Caiaphas' court because he was known in Caiaphas' household. This has led some to conclude that James and John were from a prominent family. John then used his position to help Peter gain entrance, also (see John 18:15–17).

What would you have thought about Pilate's conversation with Jesus if you were a Roman in his court? _____

_____

_____

_____

How would you describe Jesus' answers to Pilate and Caiaphas? How are his answers to the two similar or different? _____

_____

_____

_____

_____

_____

Is Jesus defending His innocence?_____

Why would he answer the way He did? _____

_____

_____

From the Garden of Gethsemane you can see the Temple Mount at the East Gate.

Notes From The Teacher's Lesson

Christ's Betrayal, Arrest, And Trial

Act I: The Betrayal And Arrest Of Christ (18:2–13)

- Jesus _____ the enemy (vs. 4–6).

- Jesus _____ the disciples.

Act II: The Trial Before Annas, Caiaphas, And The Sanhedrin (18:12–14, 19–24)

- Annas

  - Head of all _____ affairs in Jerusalem

  - No _____ position

  - Probably hated Jesus because of lost _____

- Caiaphas and the Sanhedrin

Act III: Peter's Denial (19:15–18, 25–27)

Digging Deeper

1. According to Luke 22:36–38, Jesus told the disciples to sell their coats, if necessary, to buy swords. Yet He rebuked Peter for trying to use his sword in the Garden of Gethsemane (Matt. 26:51–54; John 18:10–11). Explain why Christ gave them seemingly conflicting instructions.

2. Read "The Supreme Failure," chapter 15 (pp. 187–201) of Kenneth Frederick's book *The Making of a Disciple: A Study of Discipleship from the Life of Simon Peter.* Study carefully what he has to say about Peter's denial of Christ. List the practical lessons that we can learn from Peter's failure.

3. Write a paper explaining how to have Christ-like composure and self-control. Use Scripture references and examples as support for your points.

4. Conduct a study and write a report about Annas, Caiaphas, or the Sanhedrin.

5. Find and describe briefly other references in the Bible to the cedars of Lebanon.

6. Conduct a study of the life of Judas, tracing his downfall. How did he end up such a spiritual failure?

(Left) Caiaphas was the high priest during Jesus' adult life after he succeeded Annas, his father-in-law, in A.D. 18. Like many sites in Jerusalem, shrines have been built on supposed sites of Caiaphas' and Annas' residences, but solid evidence for this conjecture has not yet been uncovered. Their homes were likely in the wealthy Mount Zion area of the city.

When Jesus was arrested, He was first taken to Annas' home, indicating that he was still a man of great influence. From there He was led to Caiaphas' mansion for further questioning and ac-cusation. It was likely in the same place that the Sanhedrin met in John 11:45–57 to plot Jesus' murder. There, Caiaphas chillingly proposed that Jesus' death would benefit the Jewish nation. Al-though he meant that it would quiet Roman concerns that Jesus' fame could lead to a popular uprising, John explains that God used Caiaphas to prophesy that Jesus' death would provide re-demption for the people of God across the earth.

At left are photographs from within the Wohl Museum in Jerusa-lem of a model (top) and excavations (lower four) of a building that some believe was either Annas' or the first century high priests' home. The larger picture is a second site that others be-lieve is the remains of the steps leading up to Caiaphas' house.

33
Christ's Crucifixion

In preparation for studying this lesson, read the following article by C. Truman Davis.

"The Passion Of Christ From A Medical Point Of View"

by C. Truman Davis

(Used by permission.)

In this paper, I shall discuss some of the physical aspects of the passion or suffering of Christ. We shall follow Him from Gethsemane, through His trial, His scourging, His path along the Via Dolorosa, *to His last dying hours on the Cross.*

I became interested in this about a year ago when I read an account of the crucifixion in Jim Bishop's book, The Day Christ Died. *I suddenly realized that I had taken the crucifixion more or less for granted all these years—that I had grown callus to its horror by a too easy familiarity with the grim details—and a too distant friendship with Him. It finally occurred to me that as a physician I didn't even know the actual immediate cause of death. The gospel writers don't help us very much on this point, because crucifixion and scourging were so common during their lifetime that they undoubtedly considered a detailed description totally superfluous—so we have the concise words of the evangelists: "Pilate, having scourged Jesus, delivered Him to them to be crucified—and they crucified Him."*

I am indebted to many who have studied this subject in the past, and especially to a contemporary colleague, Dr. Pierre Barbet, a French surgeon who has done exhaustive historical and experimental research and has written extensively on the subject.

The infinite psychic and spiritual suffering of the Incarnate God in atonement for the sins of fallen man I have no competence to discuss; however, the physiological and anatomical aspects of our Lord's passion we can examine in some detail. . . . What did the body of Jesus of Nazareth actually endure during those hours of torture?

This led me first to a study of the practice of crucifixion itself; that is, the torture and execution of a person by fixation to a cross. Apparently, the first known practice of crucifixion was by the Persians. Alexander and his generals brought it back to the Mediterranean world—to Egypt and to Carthage. The Romans apparently learned the practice from the Carthaginians and (as with almost everything that the Romans did) rapidly developed a very high degree of efficiency and skill in carrying it out. A number of Roman authors (Livy, Cicero, Tacitus) comment on it. Several innovations and modifications are described in the ancient literature; I'll mention only a few which may have some bearing here. The upright portion of the cross (or stipes) could have the cross-arm (or patibulum) attached two or three feet below its top—this is what we commonly think of today as the classical form of the cross (the one which we have later named the Latin cross); however, the common form used in our Lord's day was the Tau cross (shaped like the Greek letter Tau or like a T). In this cross the patibulum was placed in a notch at the top of the stipes. There is fairly overwhelming archeological evidence that it was on this type of cross that Jesus was crucified.

The upright post, or stipes, was generally permanently fixed in the ground at the site of the execution and the condemned man was forced to carry the patibulum, apparently weighing about 110 pounds, from the prison to the place of execution. Without any historical or biblical proof, medieval and Renaissance painters have given us our picture of Christ carrying the entire cross. Many of these painters and most of the sculptors of crucifixes today show the nails through the palms. Roman historical accounts and experimental work have shown that nails were driven between the small bones of the wrists and not through the palms. Nails driven through the palms will strip out between the fingers when they support the weight of a human body. The misconception may have come about through the misunderstanding of Jesus' words to Thomas,

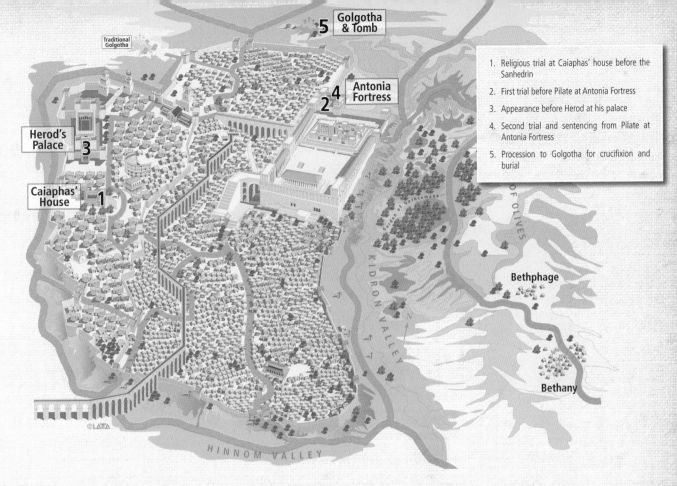

Map legend:
1. Religious trial at Caiaphas' house before the Sanhedrin
2. First trial before Pilate at Antonia Fortress
3. Appearance before Herod at his palace
4. Second trial and sentencing from Pilate at Antonia Fortress
5. Procession to Golgotha for crucifixion and burial

"Observe my hands." Anatomists, both modern and ancient, have always considered the wrists as part of the hand.

A titulus, or small sign, stating the victim's crime was usually carried at the front of the procession and later nailed to the cross above the head. This sign with its staff nailed to the top of the cross would have given it somewhat the characteristic form of the Latin cross.

The physical passion of Christ begins in Gethsemane. Of the many aspects of this initial suffering, I shall only discuss the one of physiological interest, the bloody sweat. It is interesting that the physician of the group, St. Luke, is the only one to mention this. He says, "And being in agony, He prayed the longer. And his sweat became as drops of blood, trickling down upon the ground."

Every attempt imaginable has been used by modern scholars to explain away this phrase, apparently under the mistaken impression that this just doesn't happen.

A great deal of effort could be saved by consulting the medical literature. Though very rare, the phenomenon of hematidrosis, or bloody sweat, is well documented. Under great emotional stress, tiny capillaries in the sweat glands can break,

Above is excavated Roman pavement upon which some believe Christ may have actually walked on his way to Golgotha. It is located numerous archeological layers and twenty feet below the Via Dolorosa.

thus mixing blood with sweat. This process alone could have produced marked weakness and possible shock.

We shall move rapidly through the betrayal and arrest; I must stress again that important portions of the Passion story are missing from this account. This may be frustrating to you, but in order to adhere to our purpose of discussing only the purely physical aspects of the Passion, this is necessary. After the arrest in the middle of the night, Jesus was brought before the Sanhedrin and Caiaphas, the High Priest; it is here that the first physical trauma was inflicted. A soldier struck Jesus across the face for remaining silent when questioned by Caiaphas. The palace guards then blindfolded Him and mockingly taunted Him to identify them as they passed by, spat on Him, and struck Him in the face.

In the early morning, Jesus, battered and bruised, dehydrated, and exhausted from a sleepless night, is taken across Jerusalem to the Praetorium of the Fortress Antonia, the seat of government of the Procurator of Judea, Pontius Pilate. You are, of course, familiar with Pilate's action in attempting to pass responsibility to Herod Antipas, the Tetrarch of Judea. Jesus apparently suffered no physical mistreatment at the hands of Herod and was returned to Pilate. It was then, in response to the cries of the mob, that Pilate ordered Bar-Abbas released and condemned Jesus to scourging and crucifixion. There is much disagreement among authorities about the scourging as a prelude to crucifixion. Most Roman writers from this period do not associate the two. Many scholars believe that Pilate originally ordered Jesus scourged as His full punishment and that the death sentence by crucifixion came only in response to the taunt by the mob that the procurator was not properly defending Caesar against this pretender who claimed to be the King of the Jews.

Preparations for the scourging are carried out. The prisoner is stripped of His clothing and His hands tied to a post above His head. It is doubtful whether the Romans made any attempt to follow the Jewish law in this matter of scourging. The Jews had an ancient law prohibiting more than forty lashes. The Pharisees always making sure the law was strictly kept, insisted that only thirty-nine lashes be given. (In case of miscount, they were sure of remaining within the law.) The

The Via Dolorosa is the proposed route Christ took from Pilate's judgment hall to Golgotha. The doorway to the right leads to the Church of the Flagellation where Christ was beaten. After this beating Pilate presented Jesus to the crowds saying, "Behold the man." At the top left is the Ecce Homo Arch—the traditional site of this declaration.

Above is a view of Gordon's Calvary, where Jesus was possibly crucified. This hill is part of Mount Moriah where Abraham offered Isaac and lies outside the city wall. In ancient times a Roman road ran between the hill and the city which sat to the right. *Golgotha* means "Place of the Skull." The unusual rock formations may explain how this hill got its name.

Scripture does not suggest that Christ was crucified on top of a hill. He was likely crucified alongside the road to intimidate passersby following Roman custom. The Gospels simply say He was taken to the Place of the Skull.

Roman legionnaire steps forward with the flagrum (or flagellum) in his hand. This is a short whip consisting of several heavy, leather thongs with two small balls of lead attached near the ends of each. The heavy whip is brought down with full force again and again across Jesus' shoulders, back and legs. At first the heavy thongs cut through the skin only. Then, as the blows continue, they cut deeper into subcutaneous tissues, producing first an oozing of blood from the capillaries and veins of the skin, and finally spurting arterial bleeding from vessels in the underlying muscles. The small balls of lead first produce large, deep bruises, which are broken open by subsequent blows. Finally the skin of the back is hanging in long ribbons and the entire area is an unrecognizable mass of torn, bleeding tissue. When the centurion in charge determines that the prisoner is near death, the beating is finally stopped.

The half-fainting Jesus is then untied and allowed to slump to the stone pavement, wet with His own blood. The Roman soldiers see a great joke in this provincial Jew claiming to be a king. They throw a robe across His shoulders and place a stick in His hand for a scepter. They still need a crown to make their travesty complete. A small bundle of flexible branches covered with long thorns (commonly used for firewood) are plaited into the shape of a crown and this is pressed into His scalp. Again there is copious bleeding (the scalp being one of the most vascular areas of the body). After mocking Him and striking Him across the face, the soldiers take the stick from His hand and strike Him across the head, driving the thorns deeper into His scalp. Finally, they tire of their sadistic sport and the robe is torn from His back. This had already become adherent to the clots of blood and serum in the wounds, and its removal, just as the careless removal of a surgical bandage, causes excruciating pain . . . almost as though He were again being whipped—and the wounds again begin to bleed.

In deference to Jewish custom, the Romans return His garments. The heavy patibulum of the cross is tied across His shoulders, and the procession of the condemned Christ, two thieves and the execution detail, headed by a centurion, begins its slow journey along the Via Dolorosa. In spite of His efforts to walk erect, the weight of the heavy wooden beam, together with the shock produced by copious blood loss, is too much. He stumbles and falls. The rough wood of the beam gouges into the lacerated skin and muscles of the shoulders. He tries to rise, but human muscles have been pushed beyond their endurance. The centurion, anxious to get on with the crucifixion, selects a stalwart North African onlooker, Simon of Cyrene, to carry the cross. Jesus follows, still bleeding and sweating the cold, clammy sweat of shock. The 650-yard journey from the Fortress Antonia to Golgotha is finally completed. The prisoner is again stripped of His clothes—except for a loin cloth which is allowed the Jews.

The crucifixion begins. Jesus is offered wine mixed with myrrh, a mild analgesic mixture. He refuses to drink. Simon is ordered to place the patibulum on the ground and Jesus is quickly thrown backward with His shoulders against the wood. The legionnaire feels for the depression at the front of the wrist. He drives a heavy, square, wrought iron nail through the wrist and deep into the wood. Quickly, he moves to the other side and repeats the action, being careful not to pull the arms too tightly, but to allow some flexion and movement. The patibulum is then lifted in place at the top of the stipes and the titulus reading, "Jesus of Nazareth, King of the Jews," is nailed in place.

The left foot is pressed backward against the right foot, and with both feet extended, toes down, a nail is driven through the arch of each, leaving the knees moderately flexed. The victim is now crucified. As he slowly sags down with more weight on the nails in the wrists, excruciating, fiery pain shoots along the arms to explode in the brain—the nails in the wrists are putting pressure on the median nerves. As He pushes Himself upward to avoid this stretching torment, He places full weight on the nail through His feet. Again there is searing agony of the nail tearing through the nerves between the metatarsal bones of the feet.

At this point, another phenomenon occurs. As the arms fatigue, great waves of cramps sweep over the muscles, knotting them in deep, relentless throbbing pain. With these cramps comes the inability to push Himself upward. Hanging by His arms, the pectoral muscles are paralyzed and the intercostal muscles are unable to act. Air can be drawn into the lungs but cannot be exhaled. Jesus fights to raise Himself in order to get even one short breath. Finally, carbon dioxide builds up in the lungs and in the blood stream and the cramps partially subside. Spasmodically, He is able to push Himself upward to exhale and bring in the life-giving oxygen. It was undoubtedly during these periods that He uttered the seven short sentences which are recorded.

The first, looking down at the Roman soldiers throwing dice for His seamless garment. "Father, forgive them for they know not what they do."

The second to the penitent thief, "Today thou shalt be with me in Paradise."

The third looking down at the terrified, grief stricken, adolescent John (the beloved Apostle), He said, "Behold thy mother," and looking to Mary, "Woman, behold thy son."

The fourth cry is from the beginning of the 22nd Psalm, "My God, my God, why hast thou forsaken me?"

Hours of this limitless pain, cycles of twisting, joint-rending cramps, intermittent partial asphyxiation, searing pain as tissue is torn from His lacerated back as He moves up and down against the rough timber. Then another agony begins. A deep crushing pain deep in the chest as the pericardium slowly fills with serum and begins to compress the heart.

Let us remember again the 22nd Psalm (the 14th verse), "I am poured out like water, and all my bones are out of joint: my heart is like wax,; it is melted in the midst of my bowels."

It is now almost over—the loss of tissue fluids has reached the critical level—the compressed heart is struggling to pump heavy, thick, sluggish blood into the tissues—the tortured lungs are making a frantic effort to gasp in small gulps of air. The markedly dehydrated tissues send their flood of stimuli to the brain.

Jesus gasps His fifth cry, "I thirst."

A sponge soaked in Posca, the cheap, sour wine which is the staple drink of the Roman legionnaires, is lifted to His lips. He apparently doesn't take any of the liquid. The body of Jesus is now in extremis, and He can feel the chill of death creeping through His tissues. The realization brings out His sixth words—possibly little more than a tortured whisper.

"It is finished."

His mission of atonement has been completed. Finally He can allow His body to die.

With one last surge of strength, He once again presses His torn feet against the nail, straightens His legs, takes a deeper breath, and utters His seventh and last cry, "Father, into thy hands I commit my spirit."

The rest you know. In order that the Sabbath not be profaned, the Jews asked that the condemned men be dispatched and removed from the crosses. The common method of ending a crucifixion was by crurifracture, the breaking of the bones of the legs. This prevented the victim from pushing himself upward; the tension could not be relieved from the muscles of the chest, and rapid suffocation occurred. The legs of the two thieves were broken, but when they came to Jesus they saw that this was unnecessary.

Apparently to make doubly sure of death, the legionnaire drove his lance through the fifth interspace between the ribs, upward through the pericardium and into the heart. The 34th verse of the 19th chapter of the Gospel according to St. John: "And immediately there came out blood and water." Thus there was an escape of watery fluid from the sac surrounding the heart and blood from the interior of the heart. We, therefore, have rather conclusive post-mortem evidence that our Lord died, not the usual crucifixion death by suffocation, but the heart failure due to shock and constriction of the heart by fluid in the pericardium.

Thus we have seen a glimpse of the epitome of evil which man can exhibit toward man and toward God. This is not a pretty sight and is apt to leave us despondent and depressed. How grateful we can be that we have a sequel. A glimpse of the infinite mercy of God towards man—the miracle of the atonement and the expectation of Easter morning!

As we've noted so frequently during our study this year, John often leaves a gap in events in Christ's life that we must fill using the other gospel writers' accounts. Such is the case again. Look up each of the following references and write what happened according to that passage.

Late Saturday evening to Sunday morning:

Mark 16:1— _____

_____

_____

_____

Matthew 28:1–4— _____

_____

_____

_____

_____

_____

Early Sunday morning:

Mark 16:2–8— _____

_____

_____

_____

_____

With that, we can now resume our study of John's exciting account of Jesus' resurrection!

Student Work

Read John 18:28–19:37.

What do you think Pilate was trying to do by offering to release Jesus? _____

_____

_____

Do you think he was surprised by the Jews' response?_____

Why would Pilate allow the soldiers to torture Jesus when he believed Jesus was innocent?_____

_____

_____

✎ What do you think Pilate really believed about who Jesus was?

_____

_____

_____

✎ Is there anything about his reactions to Jesus that surprises you, given the fact that he was a powerful Roman official? _____

_____

_____

_____

✎ When Jesus said, "It is finished," what do you think the "it" was?

_____

_____

_____

✎ Imagine that you were a Jew who had followed Jesus and been amazed by his teaching and miracles, but had not yet become convinced that He was God. What would you have thought about the crucifixion scene? Would it have made you more or less likely to believe in Him? _____

_____

_____

_____

_____

✎ What made Jesus die more quickly than the thieves? _____

_____

_____

Notes From The Teacher's Lesson

Christ's Crucifixion

Facing Pilate (18:28–19:16)

- Pilate pronounces Him _____ (vs. 38–39).

- Mob chooses _____ over Jesus (vs. 40).

- Romans scourge Jesus (vs. 1).

- Romans place a crown of thorns on Him and ridicule Him (vs. 2–5).

- Pilate once more declares Jesus innocent (vs. 6).

- Pilate turns Him over to the Jews for crucifixion (vs. 6–16).

The Crucifixion (19:17–37)

Digging Deeper

1. Conduct a study of Roman forms of punishment (in addition to crucifixion) using historical documents and first-person accounts. Why were the Romans so cruel in some ways and so technologically advanced in other ways? How can a nation be both progressive and regressive? Do you see any parallels between the Roman Empire and America today?

2. Write a paper summarizing the Scripture prophecies of Christ's death, burial, and resurrection.

3. Why did Pilate wash his hands after trying Jesus? What caused his wife to warn him not to have anything to do with Jesus? Can you name other famous literature in which a major character continually washed his or her hands after committing an infamous crime? Can you name another famous person whose wife warned him of impending doom? Describe each of these situations.

4. Write a one-page paper stating your reaction(s) to C. Truman Davis' article on the crucifixion of Christ. What was the most startling thing you learned from it?

34

The Resurrection And First Post-Resurrection Appearance Of Christ

In this lesson, you will learn about two secret disciples, Nicodemus and Joseph of Arimathea, who risked a lot to show their public support for Christ. In addition to risking their reputation among their fellow Jewish rulers, they risked their wealth and standing in the community. Beyond that, Joseph sacrificed his own newly hewn tomb, and he and Nicodemus spent a large sum of their own money to purchase seventy-five pounds of perfumes and spices to be used in preparing Jesus body for burial.

This might not seem like much of a sacrifice for two very wealthy and highly respected men. But consider what Jesus' *open* supporters did. Those closest to Him, some of whom even declared earlier that they would die for him, ran away and hid! One of them publicly denied even *knowing* Him, and another even sold Him for thirty pieces of silver, the price of a common slave. By contrast, Nicodemus and Joseph were taking a bold stand for Christ!

What about you? How much are you risking or sacrificing for Christ? Most of us probably will not be called upon to die for Christ, perhaps not even be imprisoned for Christ. In fact, that might actually be the *easiest* type of sacrifice to make for Christ. The hardest sacrifice is often that of *living* for Him wherever we happen to be right now.

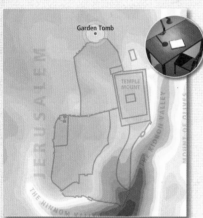

Romans 12:1 begs us, "Present your bodies a living sacrifice . . . unto God." We should follow the example of the veteran missionary who prayed the following prayer upon awaking each morning:

"Lord, make this bed an altar, and make my body a living sacrifice upon it. Help me to live this day as a living sacrifice for you."

Does that sound too radical for you? According to the second verse of Romans 12, however, it's only what we should all be doing every day of our lives. This verse is talking about a form of worship. We need to comprehend that God is so majestic and worthy of honor that we renounce earthly desires for a greater spiritual mission.

What about your life? Are you living it as a sacrifice to God?

Student Work

Read John 19:38–20:31.

If you were in Joseph of Arimathea's shoes, would you have remained a secret disciple as he did? _____

Why or why not? _____
_____
_____
_____

What was it about Mary's relationship with Jesus that made her cry when she did not know where he was? Why would this bother her? _____
_____
_____
_____
_____

If you were one of the disciples, what might have been your reaction to Mary Magdalene's testimony of seeing Jesus? _____
_____
_____
_____

Do you think Thomas was wrong to want the same evidence of Jesus' resurrection that the other disciples had seen? _____

Garden Tomb at Gordon's Calvary

Should he have trusted the testimony of the other disciples?_____

How would you have responded if you were he?_____
_____
_____
_____

Why did John write his gospel? _____
_____
_____

What about this gospel is most convincing to you that Jesus is the Messiah and the Son of God? _____
_____
_____
_____
_____

Notes From The Teacher's Lesson

The Resurrection And First Post-Resurrection Appearance Of Christ

The Burial (19:38–42)

- Two _____ disciples
  - Joseph of Arimathea
  - Nicodemus
- Seventy-five pounds of perfume
- A nearby _____
  - Buried near the cross
  - In a tomb belonging to Joseph

The Sad Days (Matthew 27:61–66; Luke 23:55–56)

- _____
- The _____
  - Follow the men as they bury Jesus
  - Prepare spices for the body

(Above) Inside the Garden Tomb where Christ would have lain.

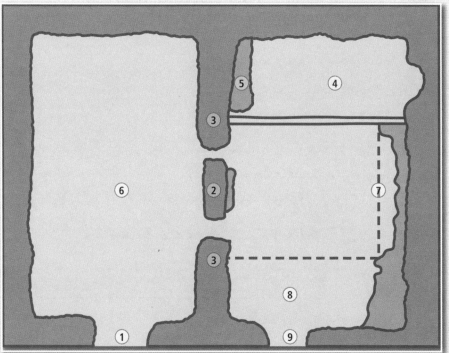

Garden Tomb Diagram

1. Entrance to outer room, hewn in rock

2. Low threshold to graves

3. Short low rock walls between rooms.

4. Finished burial place

5. Pillow cut in rock

6. Weeping chamber

7. Rough ledge

8. Unfinished burial place

9. Small window

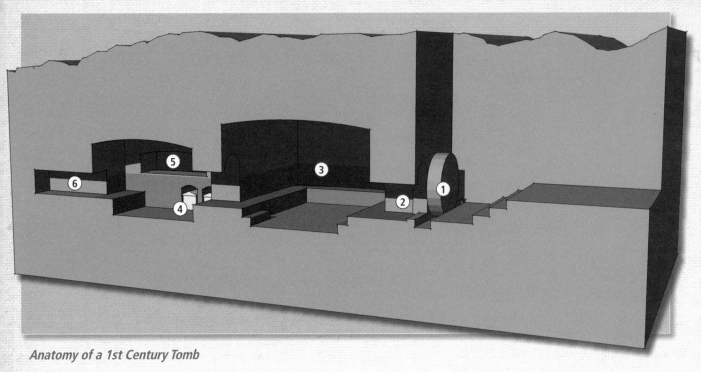

Anatomy of a 1st Century Tomb

1. Rolling Stone

2. Entrance

3. Smaller antechamber giving access to the graves

4. Ossuary (bone box) niches

5. Arcosolium—a ledge cut into the rock wall on which the body was placed. The tomb was then sealed and the body left to decay. The bones were then placed in an ossuary.

6. Grave shaft where another body would be placed.

- The _____

- The _____

- The _____

The Third Day (20:1–31)

- The angel's _____ (Matt. 28:2–4)

- The _____ of Peter and John (vs. 3–10)

- The _____ of Mary Magdalene (vs. 11–18)

- The _____ to the disciples (vs. 19–29)

Digging Deeper

1. Read 1 Corinthians 15:16–28, and describe what our lives would be like if Christ had not risen from the dead.

2. Read 1 Corinthians 15:51–57, and list the blessed results of the resurrection of Christ.

3. Read each of the following verses, and describe the appearances of Christ after His resurrection and where each took place (if that information is given):
   - John 20:11–18
   - Matthew 28:1–10
   - Luke 24:13–32
   - Luke 24:33–34
   - John 20:19–25
   - John 20:26–31
   - John 21
   - Matthew 28:16–20
   - 1 Corinthians 15:7a
   - Acts 1:3–12

4. Conduct a study of Psalm 22. Compare it with the crucifixion account.

5. List and explain briefly the evidence supporting the fact of the resurrection.

6. List, explain briefly, and then refute the arguments used in attempts to explain away the resurrection.

7. Study and debate whether the Shroud of Turin might be part of Christ's burial garments. What are the arguments for/against its authenticity?

8. Write a paper explaining the importance of the resurrection to Christian doctrine.

35

The Post-Resurrection Fishing Trip

Peter and the other disciples were getting restless. Peter, ever impatient and impulsive, was "itching" to do something. Just sitting around was getting to him. He had to *act*.

"I'm going fishing," he suddenly declared.

The other six disciples who were with him (we know that Thomas, Nathanael, James, and John were there, but the other two disciples are not named for us) readily agreed. "We're going with you."

On the surface, this incident seems quite normal for men who were used to being active. Just sitting around with nothing specific or purposeful to do soon would get to any active person. But think about it for a moment.

When Christ had first called Peter, James, and John from their fishing nets to become fishers of men, He was asking them to give up *everything* to serve Him. Yet Peter and the others turn around here and go fishing again. Did you ever wonder where they got the boat and equipment to go fishing at this point? Did they charter the boat from someone? Did they have to go out and buy or borrow fishing nets? Hadn't they gotten rid of their boats and equipment when they stopped fishing to follow Christ?

Apparently not! They held onto the equipment from their old profession when they began to follow Christ. Did they think that His call was only

Tabgha

Lake Tiberias
(Sea Of Galilee)

temporary? Or did they think that perhaps following Him was too risky and if that pursuit failed, they could always return to their former profession?

We don't really know what went through their minds, but we do know that they still had their equipment and returned very easily and quickly to their old profession.

Contrast these disciples' situation with the account of Elisha's response when Elijah called him in 1 Kings 19:20–21. Elisha was plowing with twelve yoke of oxen in a field when Elijah found him and "cast his mantle upon him." (Can you picture twelve yoke of oxen? Controlling so many brute beasts must have been a daunting task.) But Elisha "left the oxen, and ran after Elijah." After speaking to the old prophet briefly, he then returned to his oxen, "slew them, and boiled their flesh with the instruments of the oxen." We might say that he was "burning his bridges behind him." He was leaving no opportunity for himself to go back from following the call of God upon his life. Unlike the disciples, who apparently kept all of their fishing gear in storage "just in case," Elisha destroyed everything that might tempt him to go back on his calling.

Returning our attention to the disciples, however, we nowhere see mention that Peter and the others ever prayed about what they were about to do. They never asked God's blessings on it. They just did it, following the impulsiveness of Peter.

Now there was nothing wrong with fishing. It was an honorable profession, a good job—if that's what God had called them to do. But He had given them a new mission. Were they now backing out on that mission to return to their old ways? The result was failure. They fished all night without so much as a nibble. Jesus had told them earlier, "Without me ye can do nothing" (John 15:5), but they had quickly forgotten. Only later, when they obeyed the instructions of Jesus to cast their net on the other side of the boat, did they catch any fish. Only when they followed Christ would He give them success for their labors.

How often we are like those disciples! We have recognized and answered God's call upon our lives, but then some setback or disappointment causes us to look with longing eyes for the "good old days," and we are tempted to return to what we were doing before He called us rather than waiting on His instructions and seeking His will for our actions. We jump back to our past activities and struggle to be successful in our own strength. But God has not promised to bless what *we* do ourselves but only what *He* does *through* us.

When Christ called to the fishermen from the shore, "Children, have ye any meat?" (v. 5), He was essentially calling them "boys," and His question was prodding their consciences with the fact that despite all of their night's efforts, they didn't have *anything edible* to show for it. When we work in our own strength, we will return home empty-handed, with no lasting results from our labors. Christ-directed service, however, always brings results.

Greene concluded, "When we obey the Lord and seek His will for our lives, we will be successful in the undertaking He assigns us to do…Wherever He leads, if we follow His leadership and trust Him for the outcome, we can count on blessings and outstanding results… Success in God's ministry

At top is a view of the Sea of Galilee from the harbor at Tabgha (Mensa Christi) on the northern shore. This is the traditional site of the events of John 21. The fish is a Musht, or St. Peter's fish, which is likely the fish caught in this story. The 153 fish the disciples caught may have weighed as much as 300–400 pounds.

is not determined by eloquence, education, or dynamic personality, *but by the power of GOD* in the life of the [believer]."

May each of us be willing to surrender all for the high calling of God in Christ Jesus—and never return to the former ways, even when we're forced to wait and wait for further instructions from the Lord.

Student Work

Read John 21:1–25.

Why do you think Peter decided to go fishing between Jesus' appearances to the disciples? _____
_____
_____
_____

What do you think you would have done during this time if you were one of the disciples? _____
_____
_____

Why do you think Peter was saddened that Jesus asked him if he loved Him three times? _____
_____
_____
_____

Why do you think Peter was interested in what would happen to the disciple Jesus loved (John)? _____
_____
_____
_____

Do you think it's fair that some believers are persecuted for their faith while others seem to have an easy road? _____

• Why or why not? _____
_____
_____

• Is fairness what we all deserve? _____

Notes From The Teacher's Lesson

The Post-Resurrection Fishing Trip

Meat (21:1–14)

- _____ fish (vs. 3)
- _____ fish (vs. 4–5)
- _____ Fish! (vs. 6–14)

Love (21:15–18)

- The question
- The answer

The Command (21:15–18)

- Feed the little _____ .
- Tend the little _____ .
- Feed the _____ sheep.

The Future (21:18–19)

- Christ tells Peter he will die as an old man.
- Christ commands Peter to follow .

Digging Deeper

1. Explain several reasons why Peter and six other disciples went fishing after Christ's death and burial.

2. Describe the characteristics of and differences between the *agape*, *phileo*, and *eros* types of love.

3. Make a chart contrasting the strengths and weaknesses of Peter. Which of these qualities equipped him to become a leader in the fledgling church?

4. Study carefully the words of the hymns "I Surrender All," "Take My Life and Let It Be," and "Only One Life." How do these hymns express the importance of following faithfully God's claim upon our lives without returning to the former things? What steps can you take to ensure that you do not succumb to the temptation to forsake God's call upon your life by returning to those former things?

5. Read and report on Frances Ridley Havergal's excellent little book *Kept for the Master's Use.*

Recommended Reading List

Barnes, M. Craig. *When God Interrupts.* Downers Grove, Ill.: InterVarsity Press, 1996.

Bevington, Bob. *World Religions Examined in Light of the Bible.* Knoxville, Tenn.: The Revival Hour, n.d.

Blaikie, W. Garden. *David Livingstone.* Westwood, N.J.: Barbour and Company, 1986.

Bounds, E. M. *Power through Prayer.* Springdale, Pa.: Whitaker House, 1982.

_____. *Guide to Spiritual Warfare.* New Kensington, Pa.: Whitaker House, 1984.

Brooks, Keith L. *The Spirit of Truth and the Spirit of Error.* Chicago: Moody Press, 1969.

Buksbazen, Victor. "Passover and the Lord's Supper," in *The Gospel in the Feasts of Israel.* W. Collingswood, N.J.: The Friends of Israel, 1954 (pp. 1–13).

Byrd, Dennis. *Rise and Walk.* New York: Harper-Collins Publishers, 1993.

DeHaan, M. R. *The Tabernacle.* Grand Rapids, Mich.: Lamplighter Books, 1955.

Dravecky, Dave. *Comeback.* Grand Rapids, Mich.: Zondervan, 1990.

_____. *When You Can't Come Back.* Grand Rapids, Mich.: Zondervan, 1992.

Engstrom, Ted W., and R. Alec MacKenzie. *Managing Your Time.* Grand Rapids, Mich.: Zondervan, 1967.

Erickson, Kenneth A. *Christian Time Management.* St. Louis: Concordia Publishing House, 1985.

Frederick, Kenneth. *The Making of a Disciple: A Study of Discipleship from the Life of Simon Peter.* Greenville, S.C.: BJU Press, 2001.

Greene, Oliver B. *The Gospel According to John* (3 vols.). Greenville, S.C.: The Gospel Hour, Inc., 1966.

Havergal, Frances Ridley. *Kept for the Master's Use.* Chicago: Moody Press, 1999.

Heinze, Thomas F. *The Creation vs. Evolution Handbook.* Grand Rapids, Mich.: Baker Book House, 1970 (pp. 68–70).

Henry, Matthew. *Experiencing God's Presence.* New Kensington, Pa.: Whitaker House, 1997.

Josephus. *Complete Works.* Grand Rapids, Mich.: Kregel, 1978.

Jukes, Andrew. *Four Views of Christ.* 1853; reprint, Grand Rapids, Mich.: Kregel, 1982.

Ketcham, Robert T. "The Passover Lamb," chapter 10 in *Old Testament Pictures of New Testament Truth.* Des Plaines, Ill.: Regular Baptist Press, 1965 (pp. 187–203).

Livingstone, W. P. *Mary Slessor.* Westwood, N.J.: Barbour and Company, 1986.

Lockyer, Herbert. *All the Men of the Bible*. Grand Rapids, Mich.: Zondervan, 1958.

MacArthur, John. *The Murder of Jesus*. Nashville, Tenn.: Word, 2000.

Martin, Walter R. *The Kingdom of the Cults*. Minneapolis, Minn.: Bethany House Publishers, 1977.

Martinson, Paul Varo, ed. *Islam: An Introduction for Christians*. Minneapolis, Minn.: Augsburg Fortress, 1994.

Moore, T. M. *Disciplines of Grace: From Spiritual Routines to Spiritual Renewal*. Downers Grove, Ill.: InterVarsity Press, 2001.

Muck, Terry. *Alien God's on American Turf*. Wheaton, Ill.: Victor Books, 1990.

Murray, Andrew. *With Christ in the School of Prayer*. Old Tappan, N.J.: Fleming H. Revell Company, 1953.

Nee, Watchman. *Not I, But Christ*. New York: Christian Fellowship Publishers, Inc., 1974.

Paris, James L. *Money Management for Those Who Don't Have Any*. Eugene, Ore.: Harvest House, 1997.

Peterson, Dennis L. "Preventing Spiritual Anorexia Nervosa," *Good News Broadcaster* (March 1988), pp. 17–19.

Reccord, Robert E. *When Life Is the Pits*. Old Tappan, N.J.: Fleming H. Revell Company, 1987.

Roecker, Ann. *A Workshop on Time Management*. Grand Rapids, Mich.: Lamplighter Books, 1988.

Rosenthal, Stanley. *One God or Three?* West Collingswood, N.J.: Spearhead Press, 1978.

Ruffin, Bernard. *Fanny Crosby*. Westwood, N.J.: Barbour and Company, Inc., 1976.

Sherman, Doug, and William Hendricks. *How to Balance Competing Time Demands*. Colorado Springs, Colo.: NavPress, 1989.

Slemming, Charles W. *Made According to Pattern*. Fort Washington, Pa.: Christian Literature Crusade, 1938.

Spurgeon, C. H. *Lectures to My Students*. Grand Rapids, Mich.: Zondervan, 1954.

_____. *The Treasury of David*. Peabody, Mass.: Hendrickson Publishers, n.d.

Steer, Roger. *J. Hudson Taylor: A Man in Christ*. Wheaton, Ill.: Harold Shaw, 1993.

Torrey, R. A. *How to Pray*. Chicago: Moody Press, n.d.

Tozer, A. W. "The Tragedy of Wasted Religious Activity," in *A Treasury of A. W. Tozer*. Harrisburg, Pa.: Christian Publications, Inc., 1980, pp. 92–94.

Ware, Charles. *Racial Prejudice and the People of God*. Grand Rapids, Mich.: Kregel, 2001.

Appendix

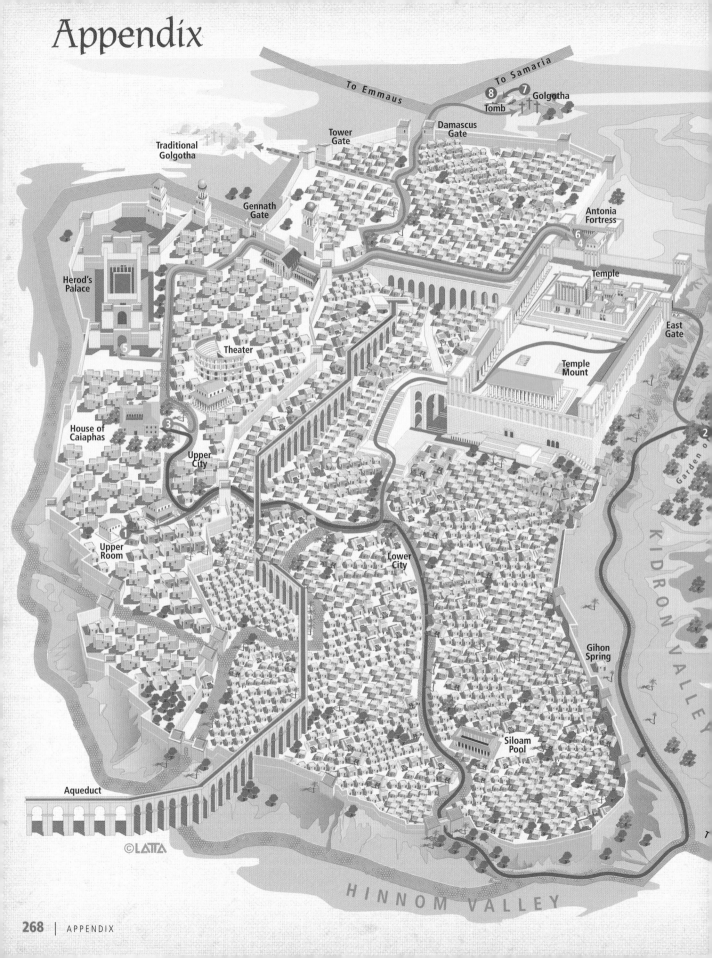

To Emmaus

To Samaria

Golgotha

Tomb

Tower Gate

Damascus Gate

Traditional Golgotha

Gennath Gate

Antonia Fortress

Herod's Palace

Temple

Theater

East Gate

Temple Mount

House of Caiaphas

Upper City

Garden of

Upper Room

Lower City

KIDRON VALLEY

Gihon Spring

Siloam Pool

Aqueduct

©LATTA

HINNOM VALLEY

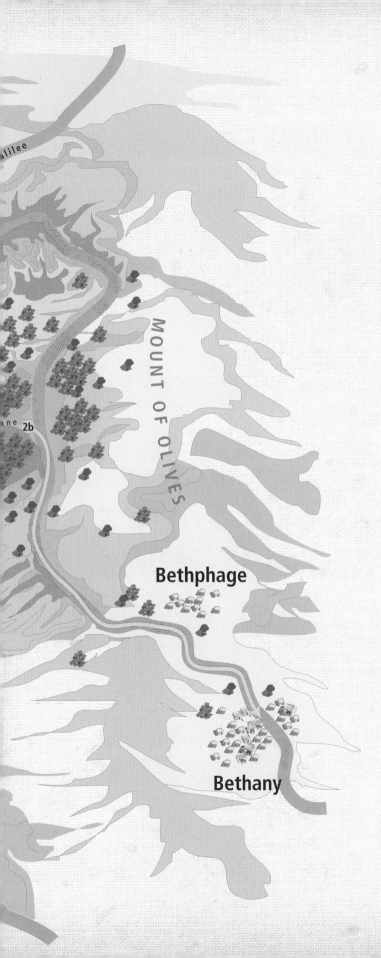

1 **Last Supper**
Christ and his disciples eat the passover meal

2 **Garden of Gethsemane**
Jesus prays three times and is arrested

2b **Garden of Gethsemane**
Ten of the twelve disciples flee when Jesus is arrested

3 **Caiaphas' House**
Trials before Annas, Caiaphas, and the Sanhedrin

4 **Antonia Fortress**
First trial before Pilate

5 **Herod's Palace**
Hearing before Herod

6 **Antonia Fortress**
Second trial before Pilate

7 **Golgotha**
Jesus is crucified

8 **Tomb**
Jesus is laid to rest and resurrected on the third day.

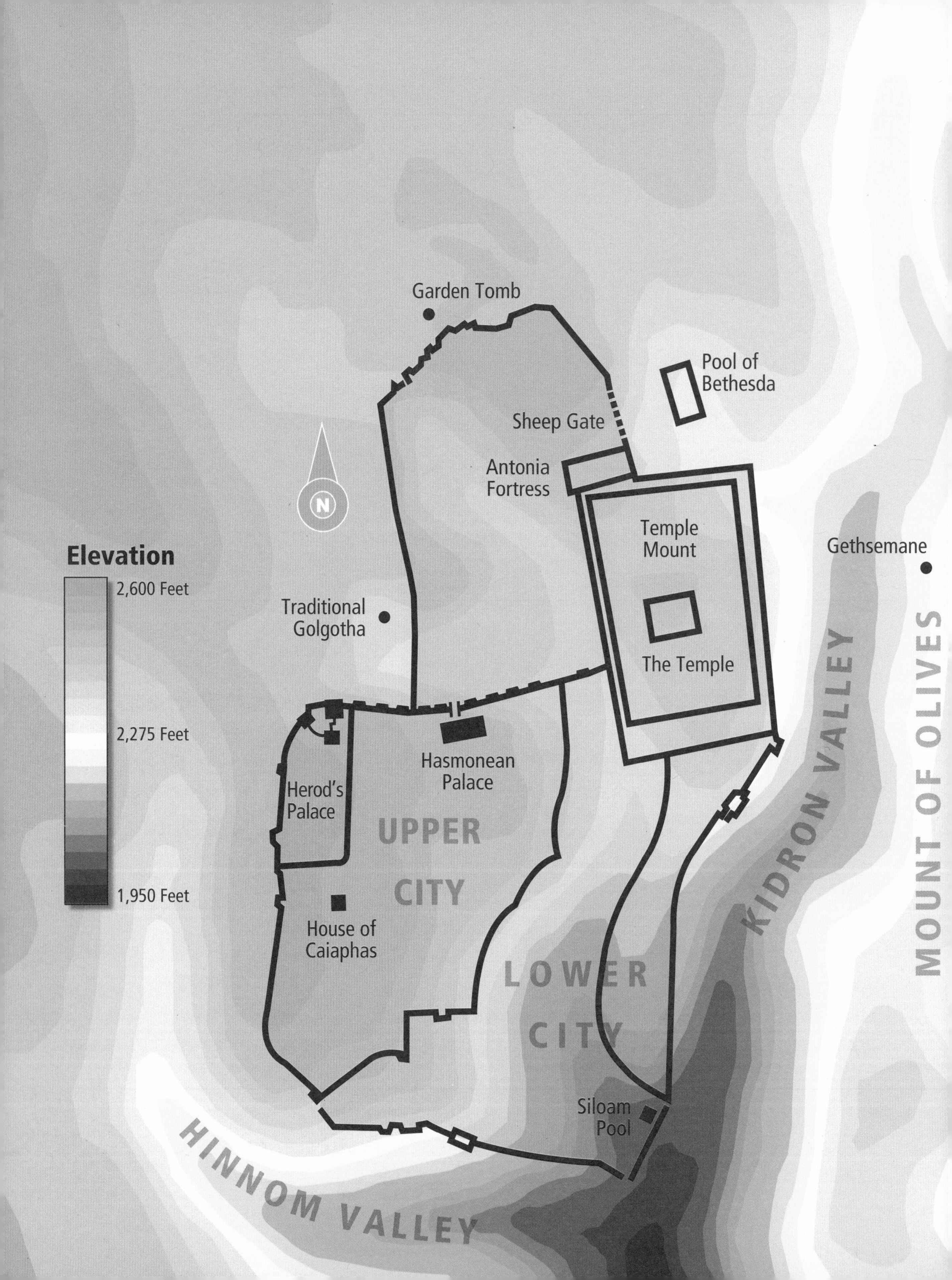

Elevation

2,600 Feet

2,275 Feet

1,950 Feet

Garden Tomb

Pool of Bethesda

Sheep Gate

Antonia Fortress

Temple Mount

Gethsemane

Traditional Golgotha

The Temple

N

Hasmonean Palace

Herod's Palace

UPPER CITY

House of Caiaphas

LOWER CITY

KIDRON VALLEY

MOUNT OF OLIVES

Siloam Pool

HINNOM VALLEY

Journeys Of Jesus In His Early Life

1. From Bethlehem to Jerusalem and Return: Luke 2:22–38
    - Birth of Jesus at Bethlehem, and visit of the Magi: Matthew 2:1
    - Jesus at the temple in Jerusalem Luke 2:22–38
2. From Bethlehem to Egypt: Matthew 2:14
3. From Egypt to Nazareth: Matthew 2:19–23
4. From Nazareth to Jerusalem: Luke 2:42–46
5. From Jerusalem to Nazareth: Luke 2:51-52

SYRIA

PHOENICIA

Lake Tiberias
(Sea Of Galilee)

Nazareth

GALILEE

DECAPOLIS

Jordan

Mediterranean Sea

SAMARIA

PEREA

JERUSALEM

Bethlehem

JUDEA

Dead Sea

0 miles   20   40   60 miles

N

Jesus' First Year Of Ministry

1. From Nazareth to Bethabara: Matthew 3:13
   - John baptizes Jesus: Matthew 3:13–17

2. From Bethabara to the Wilderness of Judea: Matthew 4:1
   - Satan tempts Jesus: Matthew 4:1–11

3. From the Wilderness to Bethabara.
   - Calls five disciples: John 1:38–51

4. From Bethabara to Cana: John 1:43
   - Changes water to wine: John 2:6–10

5. From Cana to Capernaum: John 2:12

6. From Capernaum to Jerusalem for the Passover: John 2:13
   - Cleanses the temple: John 2:14–16
   - Teaches Nicodemus: John 3:1–21

7. From Jerusalem to the Circuit of Judea: John 3:22

8. From the Judean Circuit to Jacob's Well at Sychar: John 4:3–5
   - Jesus and the Samaritan woman: John 4:6–26

9. From Samaria to Cana in Galilee: John 4:43–46.
   - Heals the nobleman's son: John 4:46–53
   - At the time of John the Baptist's imprisonment: Matthew 4:12

10. From Cana to Nazareth: Luke 4:16–27

SYRIA

PHOENICIA

Capernaum

Cana

Nazareth

Lake Tiberias
(Sea Of Galilee)

GALILEE

DECAPOLIS

SAMARIA

Sychar

PEREA

Mediterranean Sea

Bethabara
(Bethany Beyond Jordan)

JERUSALEM

JUDEA

Dead Sea

Wilderness
of Judea

0 miles   20   40   60 miles

N

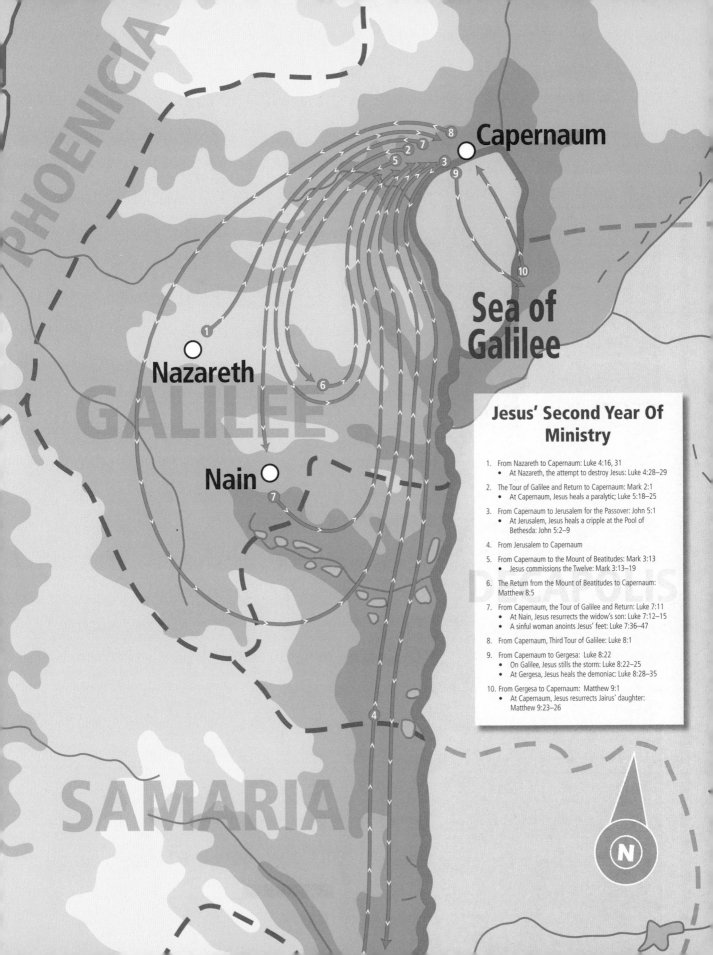

PHOENICIA

GALILEE

Nazareth

Nain

SAMARIA

Capernaum

Sea of Galilee

DECAPOLIS

Jesus' Second Year Of Ministry

1. From Nazareth to Capernaum: Luke 4:16, 31
   - At Nazareth, the attempt to destroy Jesus: Luke 4:28–29

2. The Tour of Galilee and Return to Capernaum: Mark 2:1
   - At Capernaum, Jesus heals a paralytic; Luke 5:18–25

3. From Capernaum to Jerusalem for the Passover: John 5:1
   - At Jerusalem, Jesus heals a cripple at the Pool of Bethesda: John 5:2–9

4. From Jerusalem to Capernaum

5. From Capernaum to the Mount of Beatitudes: Mark 3:13
   - Jesus commissions the Twelve: Mark 3:13–19

6. The Return from the Mount of Beatitudes to Capernaum: Matthew 8:5

7. From Capernaum, the Tour of Galilee and Return: Luke 7:11
   - At Nain, Jesus resurrects the widow's son: Luke 7:12–15
   - A sinful woman anoints Jesus' feet: Luke 7:36–47

8. From Capernaum, Third Tour of Galilee: Luke 8:1

9. From Capernaum to Gergesa: Luke 8:22
   - On Galilee, Jesus stills the storm: Luke 8:22–25
   - At Gergesa, Jesus heals the demoniac: Luke 8:28–35

10. From Gergesa to Capernaum: Matthew 9:1
    - At Capernaum, Jesus resurrects Jairus' daughter: Matthew 9:23–26

N

Jesus' Final Year Of Ministry

1. From Nazareth Through Galilee to Capernaum: Matthew 9:35

2. From Capernaum to the Desert Near Bethsaida: Mark 6:32
   • Near Bethsaida, feeds five thousand: Mark 6:38–44

3. From the Desert Near Bethsaida to Gennesaret by Sea: Matthew 14:22, 34
   • Jesus walks on the Sea: Matthew 14:25

4. From Gennesaret to Capernaum: John 6:24, 25

5. From Capernaum to Phoenicia: Mark 7:24
   • In Phoenicia, heals Syrophoenician's daughter: Mark 7:25–30

6. From Phoenicia, through Decapolis: Mark 7:31
   • In Decapolis, heals deaf and dumb man: Mark 7:32–37
   • In Decapolis, feeds four thousand: Matthew 15:32–38

7. From Decapolis, by Sea, to Dalmanutha: Mark 8:10

8. From Dalmanutha, by Sea, to Bethsaida: Mark 8:22
   • Near Bethsaida, heals a blind man: Mark 8:22–26

9. From Bethsaida to Caesarea Philippi: Matthew 16:13

10. From Caesarea Philippi to the Mount of Transfiguration: Luke 9:28
    • On the mountain, Jesus is transfigured: Luke 9:29–31.
    • On the return, heals demoniac son: Mark 9:17–27

11. From the Mount of Transfiguration to Capernaum: Matthew 17:24

12. From Capernaum through Samaria, to Bethany: Luke 17:11
    • Near Samaria, heals ten lepers: Luke 17:12–16
    • At Bethany, Mary at Jesus' Feet: Luke 10:38–42

13. From Bethany to Jerusalem
    • At Jerusalem, heals the blind man: John 9:1–41

14. From Jerusalem to Bethabara, and the Tour of Perea

15. From Perea to Jerusalem: John 10:22

16. From Jerusalem to Bethabara: John 10:40

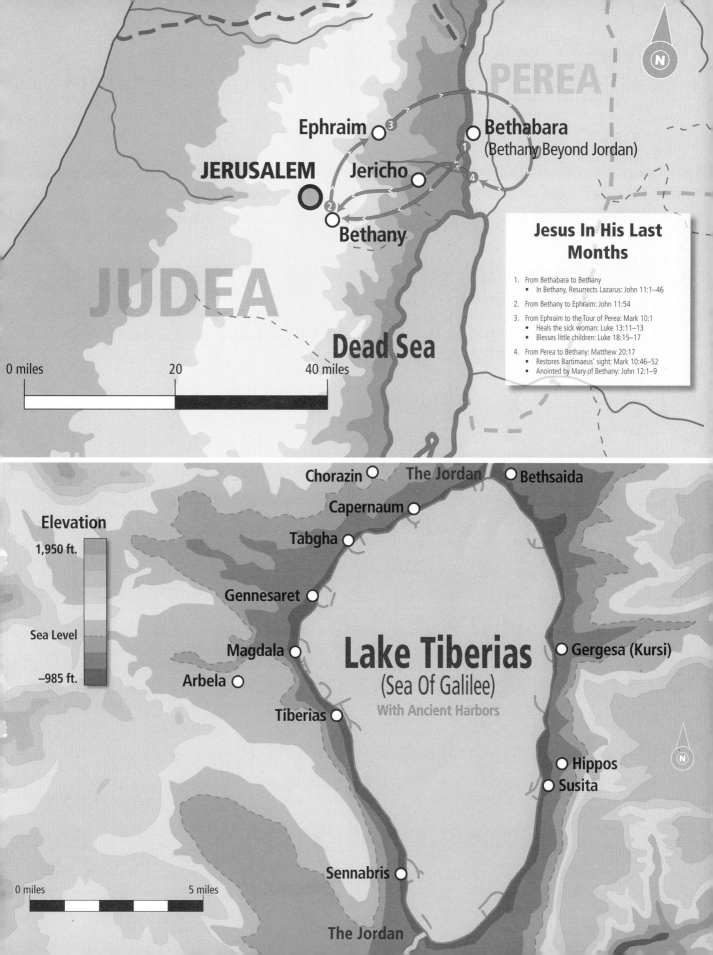

N

PEREA

Ephraim ○ ③

③ ① Bethabara
(Bethany Beyond Jordan)

JERUSALEM
○

Jericho
○

④

② Bethany
○

JUDEA

Dead Sea

Jesus In His Last Months

1. From Bethabara to Bethany
   • In Bethany, Resurrects Lazarus: John 11:1–46

2. From Bethany to Ephraim: John 11:54

3. From Ephraim to the Tour of Perea: Mark 10:1
   • Heals the sick woman: Luke 13:11–13
   • Blesses little children: Luke 18:15–17

4. From Perea to Bethany: Matthew 20:17
   • Restores Bartimaeus' sight: Mark 10:46–52
   • Anointed by Mary of Bethany: John 12:1–9

0 miles   20   40 miles

Chorazin ○   The Jordan   ○ Bethsaida

Capernaum ○

Tabgha ○

Elevation

1,950 ft.

Sea Level

−985 ft.

Gennesaret ○

Magdala ○   Gergesa (Kursi) ○

Arbela ○

Lake Tiberias
(Sea Of Galilee)
With Ancient Harbors

Tiberias ○

Hippos ○

Susita ○

N

Sennabris ○

0 miles   5 miles

The Jordan

Timeline of Christ's Life

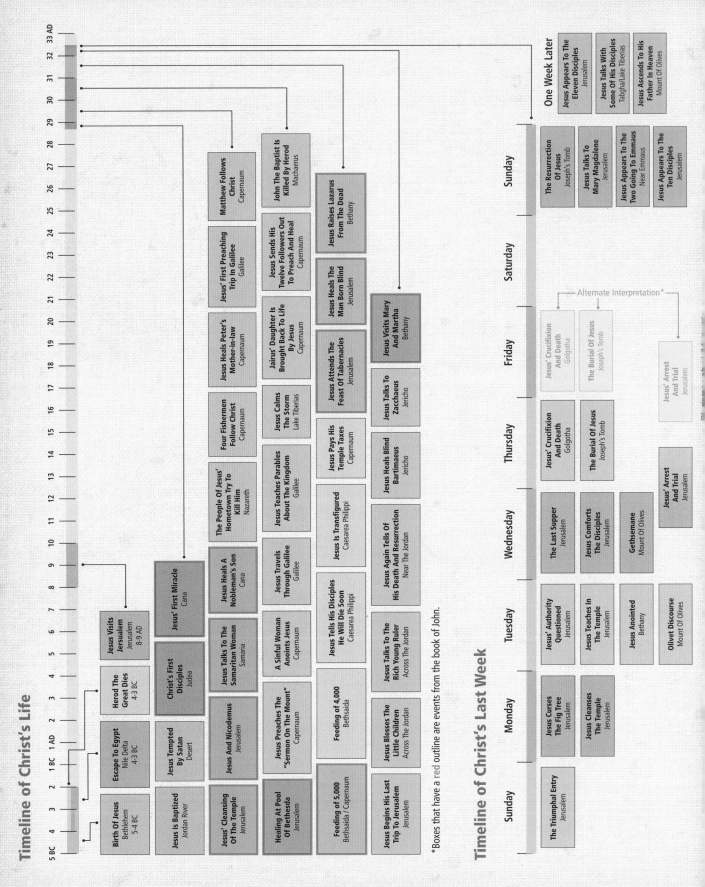

Birth Of Jesus Bethlehem 5-4 BC	**Jesus Is Baptized** Jordan River		
Escape To Egypt Nile Delta 4-3 BC	**Herod The Great Dies** 4-3 BC		
Jesus Visits Jerusalem Jerusalem 8-9 AD			
Christ's First Disciples Judea	**Jesus Tempted By Satan** Desert		
Jesus' First Miracle Cana			

Jesus' Cleansing Of The Temple Jerusalem · **Jesus And Nicodemus** Jerusalem · **Jesus Talks To The Samaritan Woman** Samaria · **Jesus Heals A Nobleman's Son** Cana

Healing At Pool Of Bethesda Jerusalem · **A Sinful Woman Anoints Jesus** Capernaum · **Jesus Preaches The "Sermon On The Mount"** Capernaum · **Jesus Travels Through Galilee** Galilee · **The People Of Jesus' Hometown Try To Kill Him** Nazareth

Feeding of 5,000 Bethsaida / Capernaum · **Feeding of 4,000** Bethsaida · **Jesus Teaches Parables About The Kingdom** Galilee · **Jesus Calms The Storm** Lake Tiberias · **Four Fishermen Follow Christ** Capernaum

Jesus Begins His Last Trip To Jerusalem Jerusalem · **Jesus Blesses The Little Children** Across The Jordan · **Jesus Tells His Disciples He Will Die Soon** Caesarea Philippi · **Jesus Is Transfigured** Caesarea Philippi · **Jairus' Daughter Is Brought Back To Life By Jesus** Capernaum · **Jesus Heals Peter's Mother-in-law** Capernaum · **Jesus' First Preaching Trip In Galilee** Galilee · **Matthew Follows Christ** Capernaum

Jesus Talks To The Rich Young Ruler Across The Jordan · **Jesus Again Tells Of His Death And Resurrection** Near The Jordan · **Jesus Pays His Temple Taxes** Capernaum · **Jesus Sends His Twelve Followers Out To Preach And Heal** Capernaum · **John The Baptist Is Killed By Herod** Machaerus

Jesus Talks To Zacchaeus Jericho · **Jesus Heals Blind Bartimaeus** Jericho · **Jesus Attends The Feast Of Tabernacles** Jerusalem · **Jesus Heals The Man Born Blind** Jerusalem · **Jesus Raises Lazarus From The Dead** Bethany

Jesus Visits Mary And Martha Bethany

*Boxes that have a red outline are events from the book of John.

Timeline of Christ's Last Week

Sunday	Monday	Tuesday	Wednesday	Thursday	Friday	Saturday	Sunday
The Triumphal Entry Jerusalem	**Jesus Curses The Fig Tree** Jerusalem	**Jesus' Authority Questioned** Jerusalem	**The Last Supper** Jerusalem	**Jesus' Crucifixion And Death** Golgotha			**The Resurrection Of Jesus** Joseph's Tomb
	Jesus Cleanses The Temple Jerusalem	**Jesus Teaches In The Temple** Jerusalem	**Jesus Comforts The Disciples** Jerusalem	**The Burial Of Jesus** Joseph's Tomb			**Jesus Talks To Mary Magdalene** Jerusalem
		Jesus Anointed Bethany	**Gethsemane** Mount Of Olives				**Jesus Appears To The Two Going To Emmaus** Near Emmaus
		Olivet Discourse Mount Of Olives		**Jesus' Arrest And Trial** Jerusalem			**Jesus Appears To The Ten Disciples** Jerusalem

— Alternate Interpretation* —

Jesus' Crucifixion And Death Golgotha · **The Burial Of Jesus** Joseph's Tomb

Jesus' Arrest And Trial Jerusalem

One Week Later

Jesus Appears To The Eleven Disciples Jerusalem · **Jesus Talks With Some Of His Disciples** Tabgha/Lake Tiberias · **Jesus Ascends To His Father In Heaven** Mount Of Olives

Timeline of Christ's Last Day

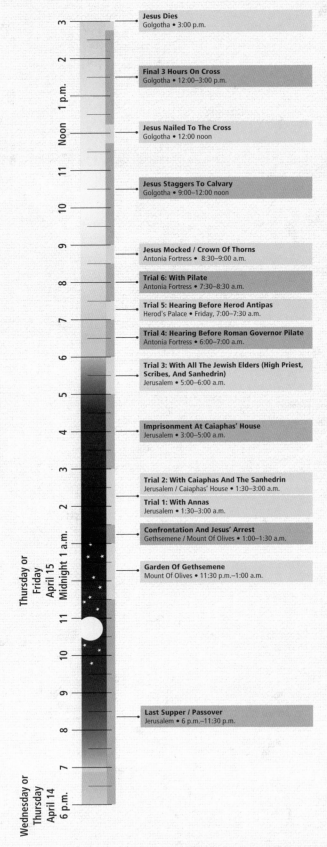

Wednesday or Thursday
April 14
6 p.m.

Thursday or Friday
April 15

Jesus Dies
Golgotha • 3:00 p.m.

Final 3 Hours On Cross
Golgotha • 12:00–3:00 p.m.

Jesus Nailed To The Cross
Golgotha • 12:00 noon

Jesus Staggers To Calvary
Golgotha • 9:00–12:00 noon

Jesus Mocked / Crown Of Thorns
Antonia Fortress • 8:30–9:00 a.m.

Trial 6: With Pilate
Antonia Fortress • 7:30–8:30 a.m.

Trial 5: Hearing Before Herod Antipas
Herod's Palace • Friday, 7:00–7:30 a.m.

Trial 4: Hearing Before Roman Governor Pilate
Antonia Fortress • 6:00–7:00 a.m.

Trial 3: With All The Jewish Elders (High Priest, Scribes, And Sanhedrin)
Jerusalem • 5:00–6:00 a.m.

Imprisonment At Caiaphas' House
Jerusalem • 3:00–5:00 a.m.

Trial 2: With Caiaphas And The Sanhedrin
Jerusalem / Caiaphas' House • 1:30–3:00 a.m.

Trial 1: With Annas
Jerusalem • 1:30–3:00 a.m.

Confrontation And Jesus' Arrest
Gethsemene / Mount Of Olives • 1:00–1:30 a.m.

Garden Of Gethsemene
Mount Of Olives • 11:30 p.m.–1:00 a.m.

Last Supper / Passover
Jerusalem • 6 p.m.–11:30 p.m.

Clock

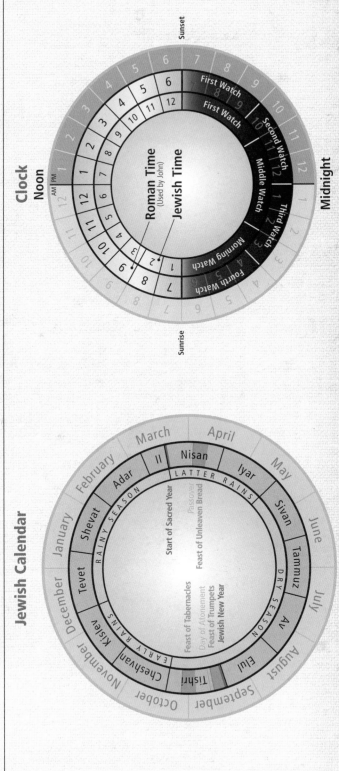

Roman Time (Used by John)

Jewish Time

First Watch
Second Watch
Middle Watch
Third Watch
Morning Watch
Fourth Watch

Sunset
Noon
Sunrise
Midnight

Jewish Calendar

January / February / March / April / May / June / July / August / September / October / November / December

Tevet / Shevat / Adar / II / Nisan / Iyar / Sivan / Tammuz / Av / Elul / Tishri / Cheshvan / Kislev

RAINY SEASON / LATTER RAINS / DRY SEASON / EARLY RAINS

Start of Sacred Year
Passover
Feast of Unleavened Bread
Feast of Tabernacles
Day of Atonement
Feast of Trumpets
Jewish New Year